D0939013

MATTHIAS STEHLE
GREEK WORD-BUILDING

SOCIETY OF BIBLICAL LITERATURE
SOURCES FOR BIBLICAL STUDY

edited by
Wayne A. Meeks

Number 10
MATTHIAS STEHLE
GREEK WORD-BUILDING

Revised by
Herbert Zimmermann
Translated by
F. Forrester Church
&
John S. Hanson

SCHOLARS PRESS
Missoula, Montana

MATTHIAS STEHLE
GREEK WORD-BUILDING

Revised by
Herbert Zimmermann
Translated by
F. Forrester Church
&
John S. Hanson

Published by
SCHOLARS PRESS
for
THE SOCIETY OF BIBLICAL LITERATURE

PA
287
.S813
1976

Distributed by

SCHOLARS PRESS
University of Montana
Missoula, Montana 59801

MATTHIAS STEHLE

GREEK WORD-BUILDING

Revised by

Herbert Zimmermann

Translated by

F. Forrester Church

&

John S. Hanson

Translation Copyright © 1976

by

The Society of Biblical Literature

Library of Congress Cataloging in Publication Data
Stehle, Matthias, 1882-
  Greek word-building.

  (Sources for Biblical studies ; no. 10)
  Rev. translation of the 10th ed. of Griechische
Wortkunde.
  Includes index.
  1. Greek language—Word formation. 2. Greek
language—Dictionaries—English I. Zimmermann,
Herbert. II. Society of Biblical Literature.
III. Title. IV. Series.
PZ287.S813 1976   482   76-14405
ISBN 0-89130-108-9

Printed in the United States of America

Edwards Brothers, Inc.
Ann Arbor, Michigan 48104

Augustana College Library
Rock Island, Illinois 61201.

TABLE OF CONTENTS

Page

TRANSLATORS' PREFACE vii

FOREWORD ix

TO LEARN--BUT WITH UNDERSTANDING xi

ABBREVIATIONS AND SIGNS xv

A. ON WORD FORMATION 1

  Word Formation through Derivation--Suffixes . . . 1

    I. Nouns 2

   II. Adjectives 4

  III. Adverbs 5

  IV. Verbs 5

  Word Formation through Composition 5

    I. Compound Nouns 5

      a) Changes occurring in the members of
        compounds 5

      b) Frequent members of compounds 6

      c) The meaning of compound nouns 7

   II. Compound Verbs 8

  III. Personal Names 10

  Derivatives of Greek in English 10

  Latin words used for comparison in the vocabulary 11

B. VOCABULARY EXERCISES 13

C. ROOT WORDS AND THEIR WORD-FAMILIES 19

D. ALPHABETICAL INDEX TO PART C 135

TRANSLATORS' PREFACE

When one takes up the study of Greek, the eagerness to acquire a
working knowledge of the language within a year or two often meets
with difficulties that prove dispiriting. For this reason effective
study aids can be of great help in facilitating the learning process.
Stehle's *Griechische Wortkunde* is just such an aid. While originally
intended for beginning and intermediate students of Attic Greek, it
has proven equally useful for those whose focus is the Greek of the
Hellenistic and Roman periods, especially early Christian literature.
Inasmuch as there exists no English counterpart, it is with particular
pleasure that we see this little book brought out in translation. We
hope it may serve well in university and seminary alike.

In the course of translation we have made a number of correc-
tions, emendations, and additions. The most basic shift is the change
in technique for signifying root words, derived words, etc., which
Stehle-Zimmermann had distinguished by the use of different type fonts
and sizes. We have maintained these distinctions, while avoiding the
prohibitive cost of the original method (see page 18).

Throughout this project we have had the encouragement and assis-
tance of several people. Particular thanks are due Professor Dieter
Georgi for introducing us to this book, which he has used effectively
in his Greek courses in Harvard Divinity School; to our colleague
Edward T. Rewolinski for first suggesting a translation and reading
over several sections of the drafts and the complete manuscript in
page proof; and to Harold W. Attridge, Harvard Junior Fellow, for
proof-reading the entire manuscript and offering many valuable sugges-
tions. We are especially indebted to Professor George MacRae, Still-
man Professor in HDS, who has generously given our work his continual
support and guidance.

F. Forrester Church
John S. Hanson

Cambridge, Massachusetts 1976

At the request of the publisher, I have gladly taken over the
modern revision of Matthias Stehle's *Griechische Wortkunde*, since the
principles on which this resource are built have stood the test of
decades of use. Moreover, it was my feeling that I owed my friend
this service after many years of shared labor on various instructional
materials on ancient languages for the Ernst Klett Verlag.

I have maintained the plan and principles of this work as far as
it was possible. In particular, I have even more thoroughly carried
through the principle of providing the person who uses the book for
study and review with a clear and easily scanned text. Everything
which does not directly belong to the learning material now appears
in the footnotes (e.g. etymological references, data about word roots,
development of forms). Much that belonged together etymologically but
was separated by Stehle had to be consolidated. A word was left under
two word families only when otherwise it would have been awkward or
difficult for the student to understand. In such instances a footnote
indicates the relationship (e.g. πέτομαι, πίπτω, ποταμός).

The number of synonyms that are given for the meaning of a Greek
word is limited. Rare words are omitted, even in the vocabulary
exercises. As to practice in the theory of word-building, where
previously only the suffixes were offered under each word family, I
have now presented the words completely, in order to help eliminate
erroneous formations through a faulty process of composition. References to syntax, providing more opportunity for repetition, are now
offered for single words. These include almost without exception
original citations from Greek authors. They are now supplemented in
the footnotes through many instructive comparisons with Latin.

This revision generally abides by the principle of concentration, above all for the two classical languages. The footnotes also
give numerous etymological references (data on original relationships,
loan-words, foreign-words, etc.) and other points for comparison with
English, besides selective references to modern linguistic connec-
tions. Also provided are pertinent illustrations of all sorts which
are intended to illuminate the deep indebtedness of European culture

to Greek, as mother-tongue of the Occident. For every teacher who desires such, this book should provide possibilities for the advancement and concentration of foreign language instruction.

Newly added is an index (D) which lists, along with the appropriate catch-word under which they occur in the main section (C), all words that the student may not be able to place readily into a word-family.

So I may hope, in line with the intentions of my old friend Stehle, that I have, with this revision, rendered a service to the educational enterprise. As far as possible, I have left his work in its original form--and clearly this is the source of the continuity--but I have also sought to meet the demands of modern instruction.

Duisberg, January 1958   Herbert Zimmermann

TO LEARN--BUT WITH UNDERSTANDING

Learning vocabulary is usually not very popular. But it is
necessary. Otherwise, you must turn to your lexicon for an unneces-
sarily large number of words. And then, of course, you do not really
read, but remain at the tedious level of piecing together individual
units.

There are two ways to learn vocabulary: 'by the seat of your
pants' and 'by using your head'. The choice is based on predilection.
It is best to make intelligent use of both in conjunction, as long as
the head stays on top! In the beginning, much must be learned fairly
mechanically, until a certain overview is achieved. But then further
work ought to be done with understanding. How does one do this?

First of all, you can memorize the vocabulary for the particular
sections of your textbook. But this does not suffice for the long
run, since the individual words are presented there only as they are
used for the given grammatical problems and subjects of the lessons.
When words are acquired and repeated by this method no use is made of
their reciprocal relationships--an important concern. In addition,
there is the need for etymological principles which set out in an
orderly fashion the individual words according to word-family.

For Greek this is especially important and valuable, for here
the relationships of words to one another are clearer than in most
languages. Thus, if you are familiar with the main features of the
history of the word-families, that is, word-building theory, then much
of the purely mechanical work of learning can be avoided. Specifi-
cally, if the father, i.e. root, of a given word-family is known,
other members of the family can be easily recognized by virtue of
their familiar similarity, which is based on the use of the same root.
If you can recognize the various types of relationships, then you
really have everything together, since the syllables are constant from
which are derived the different words, i.e. verbs, nouns, or adjectives of a particular meaning. Instead of laboriously memorizing
single words, the different possibilities of formation and their meanings are instilled in you once and for all. Then all that is needed
is to learn the root words. Thus we have combined our two methods in

the best way. It sounds simple, but how is this to be done in practice?

As we have said, there must first be a basic knowledge of vocabulary, about as much as is learned in the first half-year of study.
At this stage you will doubtless find yourself looking up in the vocabulary some words you already know. This in itself requires the
'head method', for in the vocabulary list not all the words are in
alphabetical order, but are listed only under their root words, which
are printed in heavy type.[1] In order to find the root word directly,
we must separate, for example, the already known prepositions which
are prefixed to the verbs. Among the related words printed under the
leading root words are others that are surely already known. We must
take a closer look at these. It soon becomes clear that the derived
words differ by virtue of constantly repeated constitutive elements
added to the root words. Again, the 'head method': how are the trans-
lations of related words connected to each other? Once this is es-
tablished, we may check the introductory section (A). In this part,
all the derivational morphemes for nouns, verbs, etc., are collected.
If we have impressed on ourselves all these suffixes, along with their
meanings, then for many other cases the work is already done. We need
only to work further on the same basis and we shall soon feel at home
with vocabulary. In the main section of the book (C), the numerous
examples in small print[2] should provide for solid practice in the
theory of word-building and should serve as preparation for serious
readings in literature.

And so, by the 'using your head' method (the theory of word-
building) and the 'by the seat of your pants' method (straight vocabulary memorization), the learning of Greek is considerably simplified.

And then the vocabulary exercises (B). They form the best train-
ing for the user of the 'head method'. They also show how many Greek
words are living in our own language even today. This is a further
advantage of etymology: it teaches us to understand words as language,

---

1. In this translation they are set off by asterisk.

2. Here, those items set off by parentheses (and not translated)
along with such examples and idioms as place the word in a context.

not only as expressions for particular things, but also as an entity with its own life and history.

The alphabetical index at the end of the book (D) is to help you find words whose roots are not readily recognizable. In each instance, the sought-for word is on the left of the colon, and its root is on the right.

ABBREVIATIONS AND SIGNS

FOR PARTS A, B, C

acc.	accusative	nom.	nominative
adj.	adjective	opp.	opposite
adv.	adverb	orig.	originally
aor.	aorist	p.	page
cj.	conjunction	pass.	passive
comp.	comparative	pf.	perfect
cp.	compare	pl.	plural
dat.	dative	pr.	properly/namely
encl.	enclitic	prp.	preposition
f.	feminine	ptc.	participle
F.	French	r.	root
fut.	future	rel.	relative
G.	German	sub.	subjunctive
gen.	genitive	superl.	superlative
Hom.	Homeric	tr.	transitive
itr.	intransitive	usu.	usually
med.	middle voice	<	originates from...
n.	note	>	becomes...

ON WORD FORMATION

The formation of Greek words may be arranged as follows:

1. Root words: ὗς, sūs, pig,
2. Derived words: φυγ-ή, fug-a, fligh-t,
3. Compound words: μεγά-θῡμος, māgn-animus, high-minded.

The most frequent modes of word formation are derivation and composition.

Word Formation through Derivation--Suffixes[1]

The formative elements by means of which new words are derived from existing words are called suffixes (suffigere--to fasten). With their attachment to the stem the final part of the stem undergoes the following changes:

1. Suffixes with initial vowels displace the terminal vowel of the stem; so also with final -εσ-, for example:
   ἵππος, horse; ἱππο-: ἱππ-εύ-ς, horseman/rider; ξίφος, sword;
   ξιφεσ-: ξιφ-ίδιο-ν, dagger.

2. before the suffixes -μα, -σι-ς, -τη-ς (-τήρ, -τωρ, -τήριο-ν),
   -τ-ικός the same changes occur on the final syllable (terminus) of
   verbal stems as occur before -μαι, -σαι, -ται, e.g.:

Root Word	Root	Perf. Pass.	Derivations
ἀνᾱλίσκω	ἀναλω-	ἀνήλω-μαι	ἀνᾱλω-μα ἀνᾱλω-σις ἀνᾱλω-τής -τ-ικός
πλάττω	πλατ-	πέπλασ-μαι	πλάσ-μα πλάσις πλάσ-της -τ-ικός
πρᾱττω	πρᾱγ-	πέπρᾱγ-μαι	πρᾶγ-μα πρᾶξις πρᾱκ-τωρ -τ-ικός
λαμβάνω	λαβ-, ληβ-	εἴλημ-μαι	λῆμ-μα λῆψις συλ-λήπ-τωρ
κτάομαι	κτα-	κέκτη-μαι	κτῆ-μα κτῆ-σις κτη-τ-ικός

1. In what follows suffixes will appear with nominative endings.

The most important suffixes and their most frequent meanings.

I. Nouns

Suffix	Meaning	Examples
-τη-ς -τής -τήρ -τωρ < τορ -ό-ς -εύ-ς[3] f. -εια	acting person, doer[2]	πλάσ-της sculptor (πλάττω to form, πλατ) προ-δό-της traitor (προ-δίδωμι dis-close, betray, δω,δο) θεα-τής spectator (θεάομαι view, θεα) ἀκοντισ-τής javelin thrower (ἀκοντίζω hurl a javelin ἀκοντιδ-) κοσμη-τήρ arranger (κοσμέω arrange κοσμε) σώ-τειρα she that saves (< σω-τερ-ια, σῴζω save, σω) πρᾶκ-τωρ doer (πράττω do, πρᾱγ) -- *cp.* ōrātor σκοπ-ός spy (σκέπτομαι look about, σκεπ, σκοπ) δημ-αγωγός popular leader (ἄγω lead, ἀγ) -ός functions especially in compounds, *cp.* p. 6-7, b 2 ἱερ-εύς priest (ἱερός holy, conse-crated, ἱερο) ἱέρεια priestess (< ἱερ-ε_F-γα) [note accent]
μα < ματ	mostly: results of an activity	νεῦμα nod, sign (νεύω beckon nod, νευ). *cp.* nūmen < neu-mn λῆμ-μα income, gain˙(λαμβάνω take, λαβ, ληβ)
-σι-ς < τι-ς[4] -ία [-σ-ία < τί-α][4]	activity	μάθη-σις act of learning (μανθάνω to learn, μαθ-η) μαν-ία madness (μαίνομαι rage, be furious, μαν) οἰκο-νομ-ία house management (οἰκο-νόμος house steward) ἱκε-σ-ία supplication (ἱκέ-της suppliant)

2. Analogous formations, but yielding inanimate objects, are, for ex., κρᾱ-τήρ mixing vessel (κεράννυμι mix); τροχός wheel, *pr.* runner (τρέχω run). Where -της functions in derivations from nouns, it denotes solely a person: ναύτης sailor, from ναῦς boat. 3. Profession or vocation. 4. The change from a dental to a sibilant results from a following high vowel (cp. πλοῦτος with πλούσιος, from πλούτιος, Latin natio with Italian nazione).

Suffix	Meaning	Examples

[-εἴα < ε_F-ιᾱ]
 	
-ά, -ή
 	
-ο-ς
	activity
	(cont.)
		εὐεργε-σ-ἴα benefaction, benefit
		  (εὐεργέτης benefactor)
		κεραμ-εἴα pottery making [note accent]
		  (κεραμεύς potter)
		φθορ-ά destruction (φθείρω destroy,
		  φθερ)
		φυγ-ή flight (φεύγω flee, φευγ, φυγ)--
		  mostly vowel change
		τρόχ-ος a race [note accent] (τρέχω run,
		  τρεχ)

-ἴᾱ[5]
 	
-εια < εσ-ya
 	
-της < τητ-ς[5]
 	
-σύνη, a pre-
ceding ν drops
out
	quality	σοφ-ἴα wisdom (σοφός wise, σοφο). cp.
		  audācia
		ἀ-θῡμ-ἴα discouragement (ἄ-θῡμος
		  spiritless, ἀ-θυμο)
		ἀναιδ-εια shamelessness (ἀναιδής
		  shameless, ἀναιδεσ)
		μῑκρό-της smallness (μῑκρός small,
		  μῑκρο). cp. parvi-tās
		δικαιο-σύνη justice (δίκαιος just,
		  righteous, δικαιο)
		ἀφρο-σύνη folly (ἄφρων senseless,
		  ἀφρον)

-τήριο-ν
 	
-εῖο-ν < εF-yo-ν
 	
-ών
	place	δικασ-τήριον court of justice
		  (δικαστής judge)
		χαλκ-εῖον a smith's shop (χαλκεύς
		  coppersmith)
		οἰν-ών wine-cellar (οἶνος wine),
		Παρθενών (παρθένος maiden, virgin)

-ἴο-ν -ἴδιο-ν -ἴσκο-ς	diminui- tion	ἀνδρ-ἴον little man/dwarf (ἀνήρ, ἀνδρ-ός man) κυν-ἴδιον small dog (κύων, κυν-ός dog) οἰκ-ἴσκος little house (οἶκο-ς house)
-ἴδη-ς < -ἴδᾱ-ς -άδη-ς < -άδᾱ-ς -ἴων	descent	Ἀτρε-ἴδης < ἈτρεF-ιδης son of Atreus Αἰνει-άδης descendant of Aeneas Κρον-ἴων son of Cronos

Concerning -μα and -σις. The meaning of -μα is almost always passive: οἴκημα what is or was inhabited: a dwelling place, house; it is
seldom active: τὸ γέλασμα a laugh. --The opposite is true for -σις,

---

5. The -ἴᾱ is attached only to adjective roots, as is -της. Thus it
is quite easy to distinguish the -ἴᾱ and -της here from the ones above.

which is active in almost all cases: ἄψις a touching, to ἅπτομαι
touch; it is only rarely passive: ἡ δόσις 1. an act of giving; 2.
what is/was given: a gift.

Concerning -ή(ᾱ̃). -ή(ᾱ̃) forms a verbal abstraction, but one which
has often taken on a concrete meaning, for ex., γραφή 1. an act of
writing; 2. what is written, script, bill of indictment. --*Cp*. with
these suffixes the German [sic] -ung, or English -ing.

II. Adjectives

Suffix	Meaning	Examples
-ικό-ς	a) belonging to b) aptitude	φονικός inclined to slay, relating to murder (φόνος murder) κυβερνητ-ικός skilled in steering (κυβερνήτης helmsman). *cp*. mod-icus mod-"erate" F. is often noun, for ex., πλαστική (τέχνη) art of sculpture
-ινο-ς	} material and type	λίθ-ινος stony (λίθο-ς stone). *cp*. fāg-inus ἀνθρώπινος human (ἄνθρωπο-ς man)
-εο-ς, -οῦς	}	χρύσ-εος, χρυσοῦς golden, gold-colored (χρῡσ-ός gold) *cp*. aureus
-εις < ϝεντ-ς	abundance	δολό-εις artful, contrived (δόλο-ς trick)-- ἰχθυ-ό-εις full of fish (ἰχθύ-ς fish)[6]
-ώδης	a) type	ἀνδραποδ-ώδης naturally slavish, servile (ἀνδράποδον slave)
	b) full of	ὑλ-ώδης woody, wooded (ὕλη forest)- λιθώδης stony (λίθος stone)
-ειδής	similarity	ἀερ-ο-ειδής like the air or sky (ἀήρ, ἀέρ-ος air)

Concerning -ικός. All the possible meanings of -ικός are displayed
in πρακτικός:

   a) concerning commerce,   b) skillful in business
   c) inclined to carry out, do   d) causing, effecting

-ικός thus denotes membership, aptitude, and is like a present active
ptc.

---

6. ϝ prevents contraction. *cf*. ἡδέων < ἡδεϝων. An ό-εις is ela-
borated from the o-stems.

Concerning -ώδης & -ειδής: -ώδης & -ειδής are originally root-words; cp. εὐ-ώδης sweet-smelling (ὄζω smell ὀδ-, ὀδ-μή scent, odor, cp. od-or), θεο-ειδής divine in form (in appearance = τὸ εἶδος).

III. Adverbs

Only adverbs of place have suffixes with fixed meanings and wide distribution: -ι, -θι, -η, -ου: where?; -θεν: whence?; -δε, -σε: whither?; -ω: where (to)?

IV. Verbs

Here are some endings and their common meanings:

Ending	Meaning	Examples
-έω -εύω -όω	} to be	φιλέω be a friend, love (φίλο-ς friend) ἱππεύω be a horseman, ride (ἵππο-ς horse) δουλόω make a slave of, enslave (δοῦλο-ς slave)
-ύνω -αίνω	to put into a condition	ἡδύνω make sweet or pleasing, season (ἡδύ-ς sweet) λευκαίνω make white (λευκό-ς white)

Word Formation through Composition[7]

I. Compound Nouns

a) Changes occurring in the members of compounds

Stems	Compound	Stems	Compound
1. Changes in the final syllable of the first member of the compound			
οἰκο, δομο	οἰκο-δόμος builder	θανατο, φορο	θανατη-φόρος death-bringing[8]
νῑκᾱ, φορο	νῑκη-φόρος bringing victory	μηχανᾱ, ποιο	μηχανο-ποιός engineer[8]
τελεσ, φορο	τελεσ-φόρος bringing to an end	ἐπεσ, ποιο	ἐπο-ποιός an epic poet

7. Greek, like German, exhibits an almost boundless freedom in forming words by composition (Latin, French, and English to a lesser degree). As a jest, the comedian Aristophanes put together a compound with 78 syllables! Ar. *Eccl.* 1160.   8. What has also operated here are rhythmic sensitivities (many short syllables), and the juxtaposition of stems in o- and ᾱ- (for ex. ὁ κάλαμος, ἡ καλάμη, a reed).

Stems	Compound	Stems	Compound
συ, βωτα	συ-βώτης a swine-herd	βου, κολο	βου-κόλος herdsman

2. Changes in the initial syllable of the second member of the compound

συν- ἀγορο	συν-ήγορος speaking with	τρι, ὀβολο	τρι-ώβολον a 3-obol piece[8] (coin)

3. Avoidance of hiatus through contraction or elision

θυρᾱ, ϝορο	θυρωρός door-keeper	κακο, ϝοργο	κακοῦργος an evil-doer
γεα, ϝοργο	γεωργός a tiller of the earth; farmer	φιλο, ἀνθρωπο	φιλ-άνθρωπος loving mankind, humane

b) Frequent members of compounds

1. For the first member of a compound:

the adverbs	meaning	examples
ἀ-, ἀν-	un-,	ἄ-δικος, in-iūstus, un-just, ἀν-άξιος unworthy
privitive	-less, without	ἄ-ζηλος unenviable, ἄ-οικος (ϝοικ) houseless
δυσ-	un-, mis-, in-, hard	δύσ-κολος hard to please, δυσ-μενής ill-affected, δυσ-τυχής unlucky
ἡμι-	half, demi-	ἡμί-θεος half a god, demigod, ἡμί-βρωτος half-eaten
εὐ-	well, full, ready	εὐ-μενής well-disposed, εὐ-ανθής full of flowers, εὐ-πειθής ready to obey, εὔ-ελπις hopeful

Occasionally adverbs show changes through assimilation, for ex. πάλιν (πάλι) back, again, on the contrary: παλιγγ = παλιν-γ, παλιλλ = παλιν-λ, παλιμβ = παλιν-β. In the same way παν- appears as παλλ-, παμ-, παρρ-. For δι- one should keep in mind both δια- and δισ- "twice". Check the dictionary for examples.

2. For the second member of a compound:

verbal nouns	active meaning (*cp.* c 4)	examples
-ᾱγός,-ηγός (ἄγω)	leading	λοχᾱγός, στρατηγός
-αρχος (ἄρχω)	directing, guiding	ναύαρχος
-βόλος (βάλλω)	throwing	λιθοβόλος throwing stones
-εργος ⎱(ἐργαζο-	working	ἀργός <ἀ-ϝεργος lazy, not working
-οργος ⎰μαι)	doing, acting	κακοῦργος
-κτόνος (κτείνω)	killing	ἀνδροκτόνος man-slaying, homicidal
-λόγος (λέγω)	gathering; speaking, speaking about, knowing	λιθολόγος - βραχυλόγος, μυθολόγος (teller of legends) - ἀρχαιολόγος (expert on antiquity, antiquarian)
-νόμος (νέμω)	ruling, feeding	οἰκονόμος, βουνόμος
-ποιός (ποιέω)	making	γελωτοποιός buffoon
-τρόφος (τρέφω)	nourishing	ἱπποτρόφος horse-feeding, keeping horses
-φόρος (φέρω)	bearing, bringing, carrying	δορυφόρος spear-bearing

c) The meaning of compound nouns

1. στρατό-πεδον army encampment, camp = στρατοῦ πέδον
   ἰσό-θεος godlike = ἴσος θεῷ
   ὁπλο-φόρος bearing arms, armed = ὅπλα φέρων
   αἰχμ-άλωτος taken by the spear = αἰχμῇ ἁλωτός

The one member qualifies the other as if it were in a particular case.

2. ἀκρό-πολις the upper city, citadel = ἄκρᾱ πόλις
   ἀει-κίνητος ever moving = ἀεὶ κῑνητός

The first member of the compound gives an adjectival or adverbial qualification to the second member.

3. κακό-νους ill-disposed, disaffected
   σώ-φρων of sound mind, moderate

The first member of the compound determines the second, with the whole having the meaning: "of, having, being in a certain condition."

4. λιθο-βόλος throwing stones --λιθό-βολος struck with stones
   λογο-γράφος writing prose --αὐτό-γραφος written with one's own hand

βου-νόμος   cattle feeding   --βού-νομος grazed by cattle

θηρο-τρόφος   feeding wild beasts   --θηρό-τροφος fed by beasts

Compounds of this type (*cp.* b 2) usually have the accent on the first member when the meaning is passive, and on the second member of the compound when the meaning is active.

5. ἐξ-αιρετός   removable   --ἐξ-αύρετος taken out, expelled

περι-βλεπτός   visible from all around   --περί-βλεπτος looked at from all sides

When compounded with a preposition, verbal adjectives ending in -τος have the meaning "possible" when accented on the ultima; when accented on the antepenult they have the meaning of the **pf. pass. ptc.** (-ed,-en).

II. Compound Verbs

In compound verbs, the first member of the compound is almost always a preposition. Formations such as εὐεργετέω "to do well, do good," ναυμαχέω "to fight at sea" always have previously formed compounds as their basis: εὐ-εργέτης, ναυ-μάχος.

Take note of the meanings of the following prepositions used in composition with verbs:

Prep.	Meaning	Examples
ἀμφι- ἀμπ-	about, on all/ both sides; for the sake of	ἀμφιστάμεθα we stand around (circumsistimus), ἀμφινοέω think both ways, doubt, ἀμπ-έχω surround, cover
ἀνα- ἀν-	1.up to, towards, up; 2.back(wards), again	ἀνα-βαίνω go up, ἀν-έρχομαι go up, go/ come back, ἀνα-φέρω carry up, bring/ carry back, ἀνα-γιγνώσκω know again, recognize, read
ἀντι- ἀντ- ἀνθ-	over against, in opposition to, in return	ἀντ-έχω hold out against, withstand, ἀνθ-ίστημι set against, ἀντι-λέγω speak against, ἀντι-δίδωμι give in return, repay
ἀπο- ἀπ-, ἀφ-	from, back	ἀπο-βαίνω step off, disembark from, go away, ἀπ-αιτέω demand back, ἀφ-ίημι send away, discharge
δια- δι-	through, to the end, asunder, apart	δια-βαίνω stand firm, cross over, δια- πράττω accomplish, make an end of, δι-έχω keep apart, be distant, δια- σπεύρω sow, scatter, separate
εἰσ- ἐκ-, ἐξ-	to,toward,in(to) out, away, off, utterly, to the end	εἰσ-έρχομαι go/come into, enter ἐκ-βαίνω step/come/go out of, ἐκ-πράττω do completely, achieve, make an end of

Prep.	Meaning	Examples
ἐν-, ἐγ- ἐμ-	in, at, near	ἐγ-γράφω mark/write in or on, ἔν-ειμι be in/among, ἐμ-πίμπλημι fill full of a thing
ἐπι- ἐπ- ἐφ-	on, upon; denotes motion	ἐπι-δείκνυμι show forth, point out, ἐπ-άγω lead on/to, ἐφ-ορμάω urge on, set in motion, *med.* prepare for, ἐπι-γίγνομαι come/fall upon
κατα- κατ- καθ-	down, (over) against, back; strengthens verb	κατα-βαίνω come/go down, κατ-ηγορέω speak against, accuse, κατα-κόπτω cut up/in pieces, κατ-άγω lead down or back, κατα-τρίβω rub down, wear away, wear out, waste
μετα- μετ- μεθ-	with, towards; implies partici- pation & change	μετα-δίδωμι give a share/part of, μετ-έχω have a share of, μετα-πέμπομαι send for, summon, μετα-τίθημι place among, place differently, change
παρα- παρ-	beside, by, there	παρα-τίθημι place beside, παρ-έρχομαι go by/past, παρα-καλέω summon, send for, παρα-δίδωμι give or hand over, surrender, betray
περι-	around, about, a going beyond, exceeding	περι-τίθημι place/put around, *med.* put around oneself, περι-ίστημι place/set set around, alter; περι-αλγέω be greatly distressed, περι-γίγνομαι surpass
προ-	before:space, time, preference	προ-άγω lead on/forward, προ-οράω fore-see, look forward (*prospicio*), προ-αιρέομαι prefer
προσ-	to, (near)by	προσ-γίγνομαι go/come to, πρόσ-ειμι be at/near/by
συν- ξυν- συγ- συλ- συμ-	together, with	συγ-γράφω write down, *med.* make (write) a treaty, συλ-λεγω gather/call to-gether, συν-ήδομαι rejoice together (with), συμβουλεύομαι take counsel with someone, consult together
ὑπερ-	over,above,for	ὑπερ-βαίνω climb/step over, pass over, surpass, ὑπερ-αποθνήσκω die for some-one
ὑπο- ὑπ-, ὑφ-	under, gradual, crafty, sly	ὑπο-δέχομαι undertake, assume, suppose, ὑπ-άγω lead on (slowly or secretly)

ἀνά, διά, ἐκ, κατά, and παρά sometimes only strengthen the force of the verb: ἀνα-μένω await, endure; διαφθείρω destroy utterly, kill; παραλυπέω grieve/trouble besides (in addition); κατ-εσθίω eat up, devour, "gobble".

III. Personal Names

While divine names and place names were mostly unintelligible, even
for the Greeks themselves, many of their personal names are as a rule
easy to interpret. For the most part, they are compounds, as are
Germanic names; it is quite worthwhile to pay attention to their meanings, since they give expression to the nature of a nation's inner
character, for example:

Enthusiasm for athletics: Ἵππαρχος, and the reverse Ἄρχιππος. Com-
    pounds with ἵππος were especially popular in sports-loving noble
    families.[9]

Desire for fame and renown: Δαμοκλῆς, Περικλῆς, Νῑκηφόρος, Τῑμολέων;
    hundreds of names are compounded with κλέος, νίκη, τῑμή.

Religiosity and piety: Θεόδωρος, Θεόδουλος, Διόδωρος, Ἀρτεμισία.

A citizen's gallant status: Θρασύβουλος, Φειδίᾱς (φείδομαι be sparing,
    save)

Derivatives of Greek in English

The Greeks laid the foundations of our culture. Their words traveled
with their "wares and affairs" and yielded the abundance of Greek
words in our own language. Our use of these foreign words is no cause
for embarrassment, for they are international common property and have
the advantage that, since they are taken from a foreign language which
is no longer living, every misunderstanding, every subjective coloring
is completely excluded. In art and science especially there is a mass
of expressions of Greek origin. For example:

Medicine: anatomy, osteology, psychiatry, chiropody, diagnosis,
              etc.

Philosophy: empiricism, macrocosm, logic, ethics, esthetics,
              psychology, etc.

Mathematics: geometry, arithmetic, hypotenuse, trigonometry, paral-
              lel, periphery, etc.

Art: plastic, ceramic, poetry, rhetoric, epic, drama, etc.

Give the meaning of the terms adduced here, be attentive to others
that you come across, and also test the correctness of the construction of newly-formed words (phonograph, for ex.?).

---

9. *Cp.* Aristoph. *The Clouds* 63ff.

Latin Words Used for Comparison in the Vocabulary

Through a comparison of Latin with Greek words one can account for the
phonetic changes which the common language material from the Indo-
European period has undergone in both languages. For example, the
following phonetic equivalents recur regularly.

1. η = ā: μήτηρ, māter   αι = ae: αἰών < αιϝων, aevum
                                 ευ = u: λευκός, lūcidus
   ευ = ī: δείκνῡμι, dīco. -- change: ἔπος < ϝεπος, vōx

2. ṇ (α) = en, in δασύς < δṇσυς, dēnsus; ἄ-δικος < ṇ-δικος, in-iūstus
   ṃ (α) = em   δέκα < δεκṃ, decem

3. Spiritus asper a) = s ἕξ, sex
                   b) = v ἑσπέρα, vesper
                   c) = sv ἡδύς, suāvis

4. (ϝ) = v   (ϝ)οἶνος, vīnum; δι(ϝ)ιος = δῖος, dīvus;
                 σολϝος = ὅλος, salvus

5. π = qu   ἕπομαι, sequor; τ = q before e and i: τε, que;
                 τίς, quis

6. Aspirated con- a) initial: θήρ, ferus;   χόρτος, hortus
   sonants   b) medial: νεφέλη, nebula,   πεύθομαι (< φειθ), fīdō,
                      ἐρυθρός, ruber (after u)[10]

Supplements. 1. The meaning of cognate words has often developed
differently, for ex., ἄκρος, ācer; ἄνεμος, animus; ἀντί, ante; ἀρκέω,
arceo; μακρός, macer, mager. 2. A comparison of the different linguistic expressions for the same thing often yields surprising in-
sights into the spiritual attitude of a people who express themselves
in one way or another. *Cp.*, for ex., πόλις (πολιτεία), rēspūblica,
state; ἄ-δυτον, cella, the innermost sanctuary or shrine (i.e., holy
of holies).

---

10. In some languages, the stem is expanded consonantally, for ex.,
τεν in τείνω, Lat. ten-d-ō. --Before the initial consonants λ, μ, ν,
ρ (liquids and nasals) there sometimes appears a phonetically weak
initial element: α, ε, o, for ex. ἐ-ρυθρός, Lat. ruber. --Occasion-
ally in some languages an initial s in a consonant cluster will drop
out in other languages, for ex., σφάλλω, Lat. fallo.

B

VOCABULARY EXERCISES

Always give the English meaning for each word

1. The root word of: ἀγοραστής, ἀγωνιστής, ἀκοντιστής, ἀκροατής, ἀναλωτής.

2. A word ending in -τής from: ἀρπάζω, αὐλέω, βαδίζω, γελάω, δικάζω, ἐξετάζω, ζητέω, θεάομαι.

3. The root word of: κτίστης, κυβερνήτης, μαθητής, μιμητής, οἰκιστής, ὀνειδιστής, πλάστης, ποιητής, σαλπι[γ]κτής, ὑβριστής, ὠνητής – δεσμώτης, κωμήτης, ναύτης, ὁπλίτης, στρατιώτης, τεχνίτης, τοξότης.

4. A word ending in -εύς from: γραφή, δρόμος, ἱερός, κέραμος, σφαγή, τροφή, φόνος, χαλκός.

5. What activity? ἀκολουθία, ἁμαρτία, ἀπολογία, γυμνασία, διακονία, κατηγορία, λοιδορία, μαρτυρία, ὁμιλία, ὀνομασία, παραμυθία, προδοσία, συνηγορία – ἀνδριαντοποιία, νομοθεσία, οἰκονομία, πολιορκία, σκυτοτομία, στρατηγία, συκοφαντία, σωμασκία, τιμωρία, χειροτονία.

6. A verb ending in -εύω and a person from: βασιλεία, δουλεία, δυναστεία, θεραπεία, ἱκετεία, κολακεία, χαλκεία.

7. An active meaning for: νόημα, πνεῦμα, πτῶμα, φρόνημα; the passive meaning for: ᾆσμα, ἄθροισμα, αἴσθημα, αἴτημα, ἀκρόαμα, ἁμάρτημα, ἀνάλωμα, δεῖγμα, δώρημα, εὕρημα, ζήτημα, θέμα, κήρυγμα, μάθημα, μήνυμα, ὀφείλημα, πλάσμα, ποίημα, πρᾶγμα, ψεῦσμα.

8. The root word of: ἄγερσις, ἀγώνισις, ἄθροισις, αἵρεσις, αἴσθησις, αἴτησις, ἀκόντισις, ἀκρόασις, ἅλωσις.

9. Nouns ending in σις from: αἴρω, ἀναλίσκω, ἀριθμέω, ἀρνέομαι, ἀσκέω, αὐξάνω, βεβαιόω, βλέπω.

10. The verb from: ἀγωγή, ἀοιδή, ἀκοή, ἀλλαγή, ἀπειλή, ἁρπαγή, βοή, βολή, διδαχή, ζωή, κλοπή, κοπή, ὁρμή, πομπή, πληγή, πνοή, ῥοή, σιγή, σκοπή, σπουδή, στροφή, σφαγή, ταραχή, ταφή, τελευτή, τροπή, τροφή, φυλακή, ὠνή - φορά, φθορά, χαρά, - ἀνα-, ἀπο-, δια-, εἰσ-, ἐκ-, μετα-, παρα-, συμ-, ὑπερ-βολή.

11. What quality? ἀξία, δειλία, ἐλευθερία, ἐρημία, ἡσυχία, μαλακία, μοχθηρία, πενία, πονηρία.

12. Nouns ending in -εια from: ἀδεής, ἀκρατής, ἀναιδής, ἀπεχθής, ἀσεβής, ἐγκρατής, ἐνδεής, εὐγενής, εὐλαβής, εὐσεβής.

13. Adjectives ending in -ής from: ἀλήθεια, ἀμέλεια, ἀσθένεια, ἀσφάλεια, ἀτέλεια, ἀφάνεια, δυσχέρεια, ἐπιμέλεια, εὐμένεια, εὐχέρεια, μεγαλοπρέπεια, πολυτέλεια, ὑγίεια.

14. A word ending in -της from: ἅγιος, ἀνδρεῖος, βέβαιος, βίαιος, γενναῖος, δίκαιος, ἕτοιμος, ἴσος, καινός, κακός, κενός, κοινός, κόσμιος, κωφός, λεπτός, μακάριος, μικρός, νέος, ὅμοιος, ὀρθός, ὅσιος, ὀχυρός, πιστός, σχολαῖος, βαθύς, βαρύς, βραδύς, βραχύς, γλυκύς, παχύς.

15. A word ending in -σύνη from: ἄφρων, εὔφρων, εὐσχήμων, πολυπράγμων, σώφρων.

16. Who or what is in: χαλκεῖον (ὁ χαλκεύς a [copper] smith), διδασκαλεῖον, ἰατρεῖον, ἀμπελών, ἀνδρών, γυναικών, ἱππών, οἰνών, παρθενών?

17. Of what material? ἀργυροῦς from ἄργυρος silver, κεραμοῦς, λινοῦς, σιδηροῦς, χαλκοῦς, χρυσοῦς; δερμάτινος, ἐλεφάντινος, κρίθινος, λίθινος, τρίχινος.

18. The diminutive ending in -ιον of: ἄγαλμα, παῖς, σῶμα; in -ίδιον of: λίθος, ξίφος; in -ίσκος of: ἄνθρωπος, ὄβελος, οἶκος, παῖς.

19. Adjective ending in ό-εις from: ἄμπελος, ἄνεμος, δάκρυον, δόλος.

20. Designate through -ικός the membership of: αὐλητής, γάμος, γεωργός, δικαστής, ἔθνος, ἦθος, θηρευτής, ἰδιώτης, ἵππος, κυνηγέτης, κύων, ναύτης, νομοθέτης, νόμος, ὁπλίτης, πόλεμος, πολίτης, τόξον, τύραννος, χορός; likewise the aptitude of: ἀγωνιστής, ἀκοντιστής, γνώστης, δημηγόρος, κυβερνήτης, ὑφάντης; likewise the inclination of: διδάσκαλος, εἰρήνη, κλέπτης, λῃστής, στασιώτης.

21. What is the character of ἀνδραποδώδης? That of a ἀνδράποδον; of αἱματώδης, ἀνδρώδης, λεοντώδης, λιθώδης, μειρακιώδης, σαρκώδης?

23. Rich in what? ἀντρώδης, ἐργώδης, θορυβώδης, ἰχθυώδης, πετρώδης, σκοτώδης, ταραχώδης, ὑλώδης, ὑπνώδης?

23. What do the following look like: ἀεροειδής, ἀλλοειδής, ἀνθρωποειδής, ἀργυροειδής, ἡλιοειδής, σφαιροειδής, χρυσοειδής?

24. The root word of: εὐφραίνω, θερμαίνω, λευκαίνω, ξηραίνω, πικραίνω.

25. Verb ending in -εύω from: ἄριστος, ἰατρός, ἱππεύς, καθαρός, κεραμεύς.

26. Word ending in -εία from: δυναστεύω, ἱκετεύω, κολακεύω, λῃστεύω.

27. Verb ending in -έω from: ἄλγος, ἔλεος, κράτος, μῖσος, μόχθος, νόος, νόσος, ὄκνος, πένθος, πλοῦτος, πόθος, φθόνος; γείτων, καρτερός, κοινωνός, λάλος, τύραννος, ὕστερος, φίλος; in -όω from: ἀλλοῖος, ἀλλότριος, δῆλος, διπλόος, ἐλεύθερος, ἥμερος, ἴσος, κενός, κοινός, λευκός, μεστός, ὀρθός, ὀχυρός, ταπεινός, τυφλός, φαιδρός, ψιλός.

28. Root word of the verbs: ἀνδρόω, ἀξιόω, βεβαιόω, γυμνόω, δεινόω, ἐρημόω, ἱερόω, κυκλόω, μονόω,

ὁμοιόω, ὁσιόω, πιστόω, πληρόω, τελειόω - ἀλγύνω,
βαθύνω, βαρύνω, βραδύνω, βραχύνω, δασύνω, εὐρύνω,
ἡδύνω, θαρσύνω, καλλύνω, λαμπρύνω, μεγαλύνω, μηκύνω,
παχύνω, πραΰνω, ταχύνω, φαιδρύνω.

29. Form a series like ἄδικος - ἀδικέω - ἀδικία from:
ἀθυμέω, ἀκολουθέω, ἀνομέω, ἀπιστέω, ἀποδημέω, ἀπορέω,
ἀρρωστέω, ἀχαριστέω, ἐπιορκέω, εὐδοξέω, εὐθυμέω,
κατηγορέω, παρανομέω, προξενέω - ἀνδριαντοποιέω,
γελωτοποιέω, γεωργέω, δημαγωγέω, δημηγορέω,
δορυφορέω, δωροδοκέω, ζωγραφέω, ἱεροσυλέω, κακουργέω,
κωμῳδέω, ναυαγέω, ὁδοιπορέω, οἰκονομέω, ὀλιγωρέω,
ὁμολογέω, ῥᾳθυμέω, στρατηγέω, τιμωρέω, φιλονικέω.

30. Root word of, and the English word derived from the
following: αἰσθητικός, ἀ-μνηστία, ἀνάλυσις, ἀνώνυμος, ἁρμονία, ἄ-συλον, ἄ-τομον, γραμματική, διάλεκτος, διάλογος, διάρροια, δυναστεία, ἐνέργεια,
ἐπιδημία, ἡρωικός, κρατήρ, κρίσις, κριτικός,
κύλινδρος, λυρική, μαθηματική, μανία, μέθοδος,
ὄργανον, πατριώτης, πλαστική, ποιητής, ποιητικός,
πομπή, πρακτικός, πρᾶξις, πρόλογος, προπύλαια,
προφήτης, σκεπτικός, συμμετρία, σύνταξις, σχῆμα,
τακτική, τράπεζα, τρόπαιον, ὑπόθεσις, ὑποτείνουσα,
φαντασία, φράσις, φυσική.

31. English word derived from: ἀθλητής, ἄσφαλτος, βίβλος,
δαίμων, δεσπότης, δίαιτα, διάκονος, ζώνη, θρόνος,
κάμηλος, κανών, κροκόδειλος, λαβύρινθος, μέταλλον,
μηχανή, παράδεισος, στάδιον, τύπος, ὕμνος, ὠκεανός.

32. Give the members of the compound, the English form
and meaning of: ἀρχαιολογία, ἀρχιτέκτων, αὐτόματος,
βιβλιοθήκη, γεωγραφία, γεωμετρία, δημαγωγός,
κωμῳδία, μητρόπολις, μισάνθρωπος, μονότονος,
μυθολογία, ῥινόκερως, φωσφόρος, χειρουργία.

33. Interpret the following proper names: Ἀλέξανδρος,
Ἀπολλόδωρος, Ἀριστογείτων, Βουκεφάλας, Εὐρυσθένης,
Κλέαρχος, Κλεομένης, Κυκλάδες, Κύκλωψ, Λυσίμαχος,

Νεάπολις, Νικάνωρ, Νικόπολις, Πελοπόννησος, Περικλῆς,
Σοφοκλῆς, Σποράδες, Σωκράτης, Τιμολέων, Φειδίας,
Φίλιππος.

34. What Greek words are behind these personal names:
Agatha, Andreas, Andrew, Angela, Barbara, Christian,
Dorothy, George, Irene, Catherine, Melanie, Nicolas,
Peter, Philipp, Sebastian, Sophie, Stephen, Theodore,
Melanchthon, Neander, Christopher, Basil.

35. The Greek root word of: anatomy, anemone, antipathy,
apathy, asbestos, atheist, chlorine, chronicle,
diphthong, horizon, hypnosis, clinic, lamp, martyr,
machine, nautical, parenthesis, phenomenal, stigma-
tize, tax, technique.

36. The Greek words used in the compounds: aeronautics,
acrobat, anthology, anthropology, barometer, biog-
raphy, dodecaphonic, ethnography, evangelist, geology, phonograph, hemisphere, calligraphy, cinematog-
raphy, cosmopolitan, melancholy, microphone, mnemon-
ic, monologue, monopoly, neuralgia, orthodox, orthog-
raphy, pantheism, pantomime, petroleum, polytechnic,
polytheism, psychiatrist, psychology, stenography,
telegraph, telephone, theology, thermometer, zoology.

37. Words with obscure Greek roots: Bishop (ἐπίσκοπος);
date (δάκτυλος); hecatomb (ἑκατόν and βοῦς); hecto-
(ἑκατο-); kilo (χίλιο); church (κυριακή with οἰκία,
house of the Lord); laity (λαός, belonging to the
people, in contrast to the clergy; later any non-
specialist); priest (πρεσβύτερος); sarcophagos
(σαρκοφάγος flesheater); devil (διάβολος); treasure
(θησαυρός).

*ἀγάλλομαι	The root word of a family, *marked off by asterisk.*
τὸ ἄγαλμα	A basic derivative, *unmarked and not indented.*
(τὸ ἀγόρασμα)	Words whose basic meaning can be ascertained by reference to or familiarity with the principles set out in Section A (Word Formation through Derivation, etc.), *in parentheses and indented.*
-Σωκράτη(ν) τῆς ἀταραξίας	Examples of constructions used when the preceding word itself (though unwritten) constitutes a part of the phrase, *indented and preceded by a hyphen.*
ἀφῃρέθην τὴν γῆν	Examples of phrases or constructions using a preceding root word or basic derivative, but usually in a different form, *indented and unmarked.*

C

ROOT WORDS AND THEIR WORD-FAMILIES

A

*ἀγαθός	good, noble, brave
*ἀγάλλομαι	delight in, be proud of
τὸ ἄγαλμα	ornament, statue of a god
*ἄγαμαι	wonder at, admire
-Σωκράτη(ν) τῆς ἀταραξίας	-Socrates for his peace of mind
*ἄγᾱν	exceedingly, excessively[1]
*ἀγανακτέω	be displeased, resent
-ἀποθνήσκων	-that I must die
*ἀγαπάω	love, be satisfied
*ἄγγελος	messenger[2]
ἀγγελία	message
ἀγγέλλω	proclaim, announce
-αυτὸν ζῶντα	-that he is still alive
ἐπ-αγγέλλομαι	profess, offer, promise
παρ-αγγέλλω	announce, order, command
*ἀγείρω	gather
ἀγορά	assembly, market place
ἀγοράζω	do business in the market place
(ὁ ἀγοραστής, τὸ ἀγόρασμα)	
ἡ παν-ήγυρις	solemn assembly, festival
ἀγορεύω	speak in the assembly, declare
ἀπ-αγορεύω	forbid, renounce, grow weary of
-μὴ διαλέγεσθαι	-forbid discussion
-τρέχων	-grow weary of running
κατ-ήγορος	one speaking in opposition, an accuser
(κατηγορίᾱ)[3]	

---

1. μηδὲν ἄγαν, nothing to excess!   2. angelus, evangelium, angel, evangelist   3. category

κατ-ηγορέω	accuse
-Φοίβου ἀδικίαν	-Phoebus of injustice
συν-ήγορος	one speaking in support,
(συνηγορίᾱ	a defender
συνηγορέω)	
*ἅγιος	sacred, holy
*ὁ ἀγκών, ῶνος	bend, angle, elbow
τὸ ἄγκος	valley, hollow
ἄγκῡρα	anchor[4]
*κατάγνῡμι	smash, shatter (tr.)
*ἄγρᾱ	hunt; prey
(ἀγρεύω)	
*ἄγω	lead (on), (itr.) guide[5]
ἄγω καὶ φέρω	drag away, plunder
ἄγε, ἄγετε (δή)	come on!
(ἀγωγή, ἀγωγός)	
ἀν-άγω	lead up, educate
ἀν-άγομαι	withdraw, put to sea
κατ-άγω	lead down; (med.) bring to shore
δι-άγω	carry across; spend time, delay
-σκοπῶν	-ponder continually
παρ-άγω	lead by, mislead, introduce
ὑπ-άγω	lead under, prosecute, accuse
-θανάτου	-on a capital charge
ὁ ἀγών, ῶνος	assembly-place, contest, battle[6]
ἀγωνίζομαι	contend with; go to court
(τὸ ἀγώνισμα	
ὁ ἀγωνιστής)	
ἀγωνο-θέτης	judge, referee[7]
ἀγρός	pasture, field, countryside[8]
ἄγριος	wild, savage[9]
(ἡ ἀγριότης)	
ἄγροικος	rustic, uncultivated

---

4. ancora, ancre, Anker 5. ago 6. agony
7. τίθημι 8. ager 9. opp. ἀστεῖος, cp. rusticus-urbanus

(ἀγροικίᾱ)

*ἀδελφός	brother
ἀδελφή	sister
*ᾄδω *and* ἀείδω	sing
(τὸ ᾆσμα, ἀοιδός, ἀοιδή *or* ᾠδή)[10]	
ἡ αὐδή	voice
*ἀεί (*and* αἰεί)	always
ὁ ἀεὶ βασιλεύς	the current ruler
ὁ αἰών, ῶνος	an age, eternity[11]
*ἀετός (*and* αἰετός)	an eagle
*ὁ ἀήρ, έρος	lower atmosphere, air, mist[12]
*ἆθλον (*and* ἄεθλον)	prize; contest
ἆθλος	contest, conflict
ἄθλιος	wretched, embattled
ἀθλητής	combatant, athlete
πέντ-αθλον	pentathlon[13] (5-part contest)
*ἀθρόος	gathered; immense
ἀθροίζω	gather
(ἡ ἄθροισις)	
*αἰδέομαι	feel shame, respect[14]
-θεόν	-revere God
ἡ αἰδώς, οῦς	respect, shame, modesty, reverence
αἰδοῖος	revered; modest, reverent
ἀν-αιδής	irreverent, shameless
(ἡ ἀναίδεια)	
*αἴθω	kindle, burn
ὁ αἰθήρ, έρος	upper atmosphere,[15] heaven
αἰθρίᾱ	fine weather, open sky
*τὸ αἷμα	blood[16]
(αἱματόεις)	
*ἔπ-αινος	praise, approval

---

10. ode, mel-ody, *F* mélodie, *G* Melodie   11. < αἰϝών
aevum, aetas   12. < ἀϝήρ   13. ἅλμα, ποδωκείην, δίσκον,
ἄκοντα, πάλην (*cp.* decathlon)   14. *r.* αἰδεσ-, αἰδοσ-
15. aether, aedes (*orig. place for the herd*)   16. hemo-
globin, an-emia

ἐπ-αινέω, αἰνέω	praise, approve
παρ-αινέω	advise, recommend
(παραίνεσις)	
*τὸ αἴνιγμα	riddle, enigma
*ἡ αἴξ, αἰγός	goat
*αἰρέω	take, seize; kill
-αὐτὸν παρανοίας	-convict him of madness
αἰρέομαι	take for oneself, choose
-μᾶλλον	-prefer
ἡ αἵρεσις	choice, election[17]
ἀν-αιρέω	take up, appoint; destroy (= καθ-αιρέω)
ἀφ-αιρέομαι	take away, rob
-σε τὴν γῆν	-the land from you
ἀφῃρέθην τὴν γῆν	dispossessed of the land
προ-αιρέομαι	prefer
-θάνατον αἰσχύνης	-death to disgrace
ἡ προ-αίρεσις	choice, policy
ἐξ-αίρετος	chosen, elected
*αἴρω and ἀείρω	raise, lift; (itr.) set sail
μετ-έωρος	suspended in mid-air, aloft[18]
τὰ μετ-έωρα	lofty speculations; heavenly bodies
*αἰσθάνομαι	perceive, feel, take notice of
-κραυγῆς, φωνήν	-hear a cry, a voice
ἡ αἴσθησις	perception[19]
*τὸ αἶσχος	shame, disgrace; ugliness
αἰσχρός	disgraceful, ugly
αἰσχύνω	be shameful
αἰσχύνομαι	be ashamed
-σε	-of you
-λέγων	-of speaking: speak with shame

---

17. heretic (one who has chosen his own beliefs)
18. < μετ-ἤϝορ-ος; meteor   19. aesthetic; ἀϝιδ- as in audio

-λέγειν	-to speak: be silent with shame
αἰσχύνη	shame; disgrace
ἀν-αίσχυντος	unashamed
*αἰτέω	demand, request
-Κῦρον ἡγεμόνα (*pass.* Κῦρος ἡγεμόνα αἰτεῖται) (ἡ αἴτησις, τὸ αἴτημα)	-Cyrus to lead
παρ-αιτέομαι	beg, entreat, pray; beg off (deprecate)
*αἴτιος (ἀν-αίτιος)	at blame; responsible for
αἰτίᾱ	blame, cause; accusation
αἰτιάομαι	blame
*αἰχμή	spear
αἰχμ-άλωτος	prisoner of war[20]
*ἀκμή	high point, prime; most fitting time[21]
ἀκμάζω	flourish, be at the prime of life
ἀκτή	any raised place or edge; cliff; seacoast[22]
ὁ ἄκων *and* τὸ ἀκόντιον	javelin
ἀκοντίζω (ὁ ἀκοντιστής)	hurl the javelin; wound
ἄκρος	at the top; exceeding[23]
ἄκρᾱ	mountain top; fortress
ἀκρό-πολις	fortress, citadel
ἀκροάομαι	listen, obey
-τῶν σοφῶν	-the wise
(ὁ ἀκροᾱτής, ἡ ἀκρόᾱσις)	
*ἀκέομαι	comfort; cure, mend
ἀν-ήκεστος	incurable
*ἀκόλουθος	following; corresponding
ἀκολουθέω	follow

---

20. ἀλίσκομαι   21. acme   22. Actium   23. acrobat (βαίνω), acer, eager, *F* aigre.

24

*ἀκούω	heed, hear[24]
-σου λέγοντος	-you speaking
-θορύβου	-a clamor
-μάντιν εἰπόντα	-that a mantic said
-εὖ ὑπὸ τῶν πολιτῶν	-have good repute among the citizens
ὑπ-ακούω	obey
ὑπ-ήκοος	obedient, subject
*ἀκρῑβής	exact
(ἡ ἀκρῑβεια)	
*ἀλαλάζω	shout the war cry ἀλαλά
*τὸ ἄλγος	pain, grief[25]
ἀλγέω	feel pain
ἀλγῡνω	pain, distress
ἀλγεινός	painful
*ἀλείφω	anoint with oil
ἀλοιφή	oil
*ἀλέξω and ἀλέξομαι	ward off, defend
(Ἀλέξανδρος)	
ἀλκή	bodily strength, power; assistance
ἄλκιμος	strong
*ἅλις	enough, in abundance
*ἁλίσκομαι	be captured; convicted
-ἀδικῶν, ἀδικίας	-be convicted of a crime
ἡ ἅλωσις	a capture, conquest, a taking prisoner
ἀν-ᾱλίσκω and ἀνᾱλόω	expend, use up
(ὁ ἀνᾱλωτής, ἡ ἀνᾱλωσις)	
τὸ ἀνᾱλωμα	expense, cost
*ἅλλομαι	spring, leap[26]
(τὸ ἅλμα)	
*ἄλλος	another[27]
τἆλλα, τᾆλλα	the rest, for the rest

---

24. < ἀκ-ούσ-ῐω have a sharp ear; acoustic   25. neuralgia (νευρᾶ) 26. < ἅλῐομαι, salio, assail, *F* saillir 27. alius, alias

ἄλλο τι (ἤ)	is it not so?[28]
ἄλλως	otherwise, else; wrongly (both otherwise...and)
ἄλλως τε...καί	especially, above all
ἄλλοτε	at another time
ἄλλῃ (ἄλλοσε, ἄλλοθι, ἄλλοθεν)	elsewhere, otherwise
ἀλλά	but
ἀλλά...γάρ	but really, certainly
ἀλλοῖος	different, other
ἀλλότριος (ἀλλοτριόω)	belonging to another, foreign
ἀλλάττω (ἡ ἀλλαγή)	change; depart
ἀπ-αλλάττω	remove oneself; set free
-σε φόβον (ἡ ἀπαλλαγή)	-free you from fear
δι-, κατ-, συν- αλλάττω	reconcile
-σε τῷ φίλῳ (ἡ διαλλαγή, καταλλαγή, συναλλαγή)	-you with your friend
*ὁ ἅλς, ἁλός	salt[29]
ἡ ἅλς	the sea
ἁλιεύς	fisherman
*τὸ ἄλσος	(sacred) grove
*ἄλφιτον	(usu. pl.) meal, bread
*ἡ ἀλώπηξ, -εκος	fox[30]
*ἅμα	at the same time, with[31]
ἅμ' ἔῳ	at dawn
ἅμα τε...καί	no sooner than
ἅμα πορευόμενοι	during the march
ἄμαξα	cart, wagon
ἡ ἅμιλλα	contest, conflict
ἁμιλλάομαι	compete, strive

28. nonne   29. sal   30. vulpes, wolf   31. < σαμ-α
G samt, semel, simul

*ἁμαρτάνω	miss the mark, err; sin
–λέοντος	–miss the lion
–λέγων	–speak falsely
τὸ ἁμάρτημα, ἡ ἁμαρτίᾱ	mistake; sin
*ἀμβλύς	blunt
*ἀμείβω	change, exchange
ἀμείβομαι	do differently, answer
*ἡ ἄμπελος	vine, grapevine
*ἀμῡ́νω	defend, ward off
–πολεμίους νεῶν	–enemies from the ships
–τοῖς φίλοις	–help one's friends
ἀμῡ́νομαι	defend oneself against
–ὑμᾶς	–you
*ἀμφί	about, around (acc.); on both sides (dat.); for the sake of (gen.)
οἱ – Λεωνίδαν	–those around Leonidas
–τὴν πόλιν	–around the city
ἄμφω and ἀμφότεροι	both[32]
ἀμφοτέρω–θεν	on both sides
(ἀμφοτέρωσε, ἀμφοτέρωθι)	
ἀμφισ–βητέω	(go in two directions); disagree with
*ἄν	(a conditional particle)
	1. in main clauses:
εἴχετε ἄν	you would have
ἔπαισεν ἄν	he probably struck
εἶδες ἄν	you should have been able to see
εἴποι ἄν τις	one might say
	2. in subordinate clauses:
ὃς ἄν	whoever (rel. clauses of purpose, result, or condition)
	3. also with the inf. and ptc. to express potentiality
ᾱ̓́ν = ἐάν	if (see εἰ)
*ἀνά	up, throughout, upon
–νύκτα	–all night through
ἄνω	above, upwards

---

32. ambo

(ἄνω-θεν)	
*ἀνάγκη	necessity, compulsion
ἀναγκαῖος	compelling, necessary; kindred
ἀναγκάζω	compel
*ἄνεμος	wind[33]
(ἀνεμόεις)	
*ἄνευ	without, except, besides
-ἐμοῦ	-without me
*ἀνήρ, ἀνδρός	husband, man
ἀνδρεῖος	courageous, manly
ἀνδρείᾱ	courage, manliness
ὁ ἀνδριᾱ́ς, ἄντος	statue
ἀνδρά-ποδον	slave[34]
ἀνδραποδίζω	enslave
*τὸ ἄνθος	blossom, flower[35]
*ἄνθρωπος	man, humankind
ἀνθρώπινος and ἀνθρώπειος	human[36]
*ἀνῑ́ᾱ	trouble, distress
ἀνῑάω	trouble, distress
ἀνῑαρός	troublesome, distressing
*ἀνοίγνυμι and ἀνοίγω	open
*ἀντί	instead of, in exchange for, opposed to[37]
ἀντίος, ἐναντίος	set against; opponent
τοὐναντίον	on the contrary
ἐν-αντιόομαι	set oneself against
(ἀπ-) αντάω	meet
*ἄντρον	cave, cavern
(ἀντρώδης)	
*ἀνύω and ἀνύτω	complete
(ἡ ἄνυσις)	
*ἄξιος	worthy, worth
-εῖ ἐπαινέσαι	-you are worthy of praise
-πολλοῦ τῇ πόλει	-the city is worth much
(ἀν-άξιος)	

---

33. anemone; anima, F âme   34. πούς; cp. mancipium   35.
anthology   36. anthropology   37. antithesis (τίθημι), ante

ἀξιόω	esteem worthy; order, request; think
ἀξίᾱ	worth; service
τὸ ἀξίωμα	reputation[38]
ἡ ἀξίωσις	valuation
ἀξιό-λογος	worthy of mention, remarkable
ἀξιό-χρεως	worth considering, sufficient[39]
*ἀπαλός	fresh, gentle, delicate
*ἀπάτη	deceit
(ἐξ-)απατάω	deceive, seduce
*ἀπειλή	threat; boast
ἀπειλέω	threaten; boast
*ἁπλόος	simple, single
(ἁπλοῦς)	
*ἀπό	away from, since, on account of
ἀφ᾽ οὗ	since then
οἱ ἀπὸ φιλοσοφίας	philosophers
*ἀπο-διδράσκω	flee, run away from
-δεσπότην	-a tyrant
(ἡ ἀπόδρασις)	
*ἀπο-λαύω	enjoy
-τοῦ βίου	-life
(ἡ ἀπόλαυσις)	
*ἅπτω	fasten upon; kindle
ἅπτομαι	cling to, touch, grasp
-τῆς χειρός	-one's hand
συνάπτω μάχην	begin a battle
-τῷ πολεμίῳ	-with the enemy
*ἄρα	then, just now, for (*often not to be translated*)
εἰ ἄρα	if by chance
εἰ μὴ ἄρα	unless perhaps
*ἆρα (*interrogative particle*)[40]	
ἆρα λέγετε	will you speak?
ἆρ᾽ οὐ λέγετε	you will speak, won't you?

---

38. axiom   39. χρείᾱ   40. < ἦ ἄρα

ἄρα μὴ λέγετε	you will not speak, will you?
ἄρτι	just now
ἀραρίσκω	join, fit together[41]
ἄρθρον	a joint
*ἀρά	prayer, vow
ἀράομαι	pray, vow
*ἄργυρος	silver[42]
ἀργυροῦς	of silver
ἀργύριον	silver coin, money
ἐν-αργής	clear, visible, distinct
*ἀρέσκω	please, befriend
*ἀρετή	excellence, virtue, valor
ἄριστος	best, noblest, most valiant[43]
(ἀριστεύω)	
ἀριστεῖον	prize of the bravest (*always in pl.*)
*ἀριθμός	number, numbering
ἀν-άριθμος	innumerable
ἀριθμέω	count, number
(ἀριθμητικός)[44]	
*ἀριστερός	left; on the left; ominous[45]
*ἄριστον	breakfast[46]
ἀριστάω	eat breakfast
*ἀρκέω *and* ἐπ-αρκέω	be strong enough, suffice[47]
αὐτ-άρκης	self-sufficient, independent
(ἡ αὐτάρκεια)	
*ὁ, ἡ ἄρκτος	bear; Ursus Major; the North[48]
*τὸ ἄρμα	chariot
ἡ ἁρμάμαξα	an eastern covered carriage
*ἁρμόττω (ἁρμόζω)	fit, join together
ἁρμοστής	governor, one who arranges
ἁρμονία	joint; harmony

---

41. arma, ars 42. argentum (*F* argent), arguo (to argue)
actually make clear 43. aristo-cracy (τὸ κράτος)
44. arithmetic 45. *cp.* sinister, laevus 46. *Hom.* ἦρι
early, *and* ἔδω eat 47. arceo, arx 48. ursus

*ἀρνέομαι	refuse, deny
-ὡς οὐ πέπτωκα *or* μὴ πεπτωκέναι	-that I have fallen
(ἡ ἄρνησις)	
*ἀρόω	plough[49]
(ἀροτήρ *and* ἀρότης)	
ἄροτρον	plough
ἡ ἄρουρα	arable land
*ἀρπάζω	snatch, rob
(ἀρπακτήρ, ἀρπαγή)	
δι-αρπάζω	plunder[50]
*ἄρρην, ενος	male, masculine; strong
*ἄρτος	bread
*ἄρχω	begin; rule (*usu. with gen.*)
-βαρβάρων	-rule over the barbarians
ἄρχομαι λόγου	begin my speech
-λέγων	-speaking
ἄρχων, οντος	ruler, chief officer
ἀρχή	beginning, rule, office
(ἀν-αρχίᾱ, μον-αρχίᾱ, ὀλιγ-αρχίᾱ)[51]	
ἀρχεῖον	public building[52]
ἀρχήν	at first, above all
ἀρχαῖος	(from the beginning) ancient[53]
ὑπ-άρχω	begin, belong to, be
*ἀσκέω	exercise, practice
(ἡ ἄσκησις)[54]	
*ἀσκός	wineskin
*ἀσπάζομαι	welcome, embrace
ἀσπαστός *and* ἀσπάσιος	welcome
*ἡ ἀσπίς, ίδος	shield
(ἀσπίδιον)	
*ὁ ἀστήρ *and* τὸ ἄστρον	star, meteor[55]
ἀστράπτει	lightning strikes

---

49. aro, arator, aratrum, arvum 50. rapio, diripio
51. anarchy, monarchy, oligarchy 52. archive 53. archeology 54. ascetic 55. stella < sterla

ἀστραπή	lightning
*τὸ ἄστυ, εως	city, town
ἀστός	townsman
ἀστεῖος	(of the town), elegant[56]
*ἄτε	just as, as if, inasmuch as[57]
*ἄτη	delusion, sin, ruin
*αὖ *and* αὖθις	back, again, in turn[58]
*αὐλή	court, courtyard; stable; hall[59]
αὐλίζομαι	lie out (in the courtyard) at night; to encamp
*αὐλός	flute
αὐλέω	play the flute
(ἡ αὔλησις, ὁ αὐλητής, τὸ αὔλημα)	
*αὐξάνω (αὔξω)	increase[60]
(ἡ αὔξησις)	
*αὐτός	1. self
ὁ αὐτός	the same
ὁ βασιλευς αὐτός	the king himself
ὁ αὐτὸς βασιλεύς	the same king
καὶ αὐτός	likewise (et ipse)
αὐτοῖς ἀνδράσιν	together with the men
τὰ αὐτὰ ἄλλοις	the same as the others
αὐτοῦ	on the spot, just there, here
(αὐτό-θι, -θεν, -σε)	
αὐτίκα	at once, immediately
αὔτως	even so, just so
ὡς-αύτως	in like manner
αὐτό-ματος	self-moving[61]
αὐτό-μολος	going of oneself; a deserter[62]
(αὐτομολίᾱ, αὐτομολέω)	

---

56. *cp.* ἄγροικος   57. *neuter pl. of* ὅστε   58. aut, *F* ou
59. aula   60. augeo, auxilium   61. automatic   62. *Hom.*
aor. μολεῖν go

*αὐτός	2. him, her (*all cases except nom.*)
φιλέω αὐτόν	I love him, amo eum
*ὁ αὐχήν, ένος	neck, throat
*τὸ ἄχθος	weight, burden
ἄχθομαι	be burdened, be weighted down
-ὁρῶν	-be unwilling to see

B

*τὸ βάθος	depth, height[1]
βαθύς	deep, high
(ἡ βαθύτης)	
*βαίνω	go[2]
βατός *and* βάσιμος	passable
ἄ-βατος, δύσ-β.	impassable
ἡ βάσις, εως	step, stepping; ground; pedestal
τὸ βῆμα	step, pace; platform
βάδην	in step, step by step
βαδίζω	step, pace, walk
βιβάζω	cause to go up, lift up
ἀνα-βαίνω	go up, forward; mount
δια-βαίνω	step through, mount
παρα-βαίνω	overstep, go beside
(ἡ παράβασις)	
συμ-βαίνει	it happens that
βέβαιος[3]	secure, steady, sure
βεβαιόω	confirm, establish, make secure
(ἡ βεβαιότης)	
ὁ ἐπι-βάτης	one who embarks, soldier, warrior
πρό-βατον	sheep, cattle (*usu. pl.*)
βωμός	altar
*βακτηρίᾱ *and* βάκτρον	staff[4]

---

1. *cp*. altus, altitudo   2. *r*. βα-, (βαν-), βη-, βω; venio
3. *Hom. pf*. βέβαα stand fast   4. baculum; bacteria

*βάλλω	throw, strike[5]
τὸ βέλος	anything thrown, arrow
βολή	a throw, stroke
ἀπο-βάλλω	throw away, lose
δια-βάλλω	throw over *or* across; slander, mislead
δια-βολή	false accusation, slander
διά-βολος	accuser, slanderer[6]
εἰσ-, ἐμ-βάλλω (εἰσβολή)	throw in(to), go into, invade; encounter
ἐκ-βάλλω (ἐκβολή)	throw out, banish, remove
-τῆς τιμῆς	-from office
μετα-βάλλω (μετα-βολή)	turn, change
παρα-βάλλω	throw beside, put before; venture
παρα-βάλλομαι [τὴν ψυχήν]	stake one's life upon a [single throw (of the dice)]
παρα-βολή	parable, comparison, (throw beyond the mark)
ὑπερ-βάλλω	overdo, outdo
ὑπερ-βολή	excess, delay
τὸ πρό-βλημα	(that held before one) shelter, protection, pretext, excuse; (that put before one) proposition, issue, problem
σύμ-βολον	badge, sign; treaty[7]
*βάπτω *and* βαπτίζω (ὁ βαπτιστής τὸ βάπτισμα)[8]	dip under
*βάρβαρος	not Greek-speaking, barbarian[9]
*τὸ βάρος	heaviness[10]
βαρύς (βαρύνω, ἡ βαρύτης)	heavy

---

5. *r.* βελ-, βολ-, βαλ-, βλη- 6. *Spanish* diablo, devil
7. symbol 8. baptism 9. < βάλβαλος, *cp.* balbus;
F barbare, Berber 10. gravis, grief

34

*βασιλεύς	king, ruler
(βασιλικός, βασιλεύω)	
βασίλεια	queen
τὰ βασίλεια	royal palace
ἡ βασιλείᾱ	kingdom, monarchy
*βίᾱ	violence, force, act of violence, crime
βίαιος	violent
βιάζομαι	force, violate
*ἡ βίβλος	bark of the papyrus plant, paper, book[11]
*βίος	life, living[12]
βιόω and βιοτεύω	live
*βλάπτω	hinder, harm
-τοὺς πολεμίους	-the enemies
βλάβη	harm
βλαβερός	harmful
ἀ-βλαβής	unharmed, harmless
*βλαστάνω	sprout
(τὸ βλάστημα)	
*βλάσφημος	slanderous, profane
(βλασφημίᾱ, βλασφημέω) [13]	
*βλέπω	look, see
ἀπο-βλέπω	look at an object steadfastly (to the exclusion of others)
βλέφαρον	an eyelid, eye
*βοή	cry, shout
βοάω	cry, shout
βοηθέω	help, assist, come to the rescue[14]
βοήθεια	help
*βορά	food, meat
βιβρώσκω	eat[15]
βρωτός	edible
ἡ βρῶσις	meat, nourishment

---

11. Bible   12. vivere; bio-   13. blasphemy   14. θέω
15. vorare

*ὁ βορέας, ου *and* βορρᾶς, ᾶ	northwind, north
*βόσκω	pasture, feed
τὸ βόσκημα	herd of cattle or sheep; food
*ὁ βότρυς, υος	cluster of grapes
*βούλομαι	will, wish
ὁ βουλόμενος	one who wishes[16]
ἐμοὶ βουλομένῳ ἐστί	it is according to my wish
βουλή	will, plan, counsel; council
βουλεύω	take counsel, consider
(ὁ βουλευτής)	
βουλεύομαι	take counsel with oneself, be determined
τὸ βούλευμα	plan, design
βουλευτήριον	courthouse, council chamber
ἐπι-βουλεύω	lay plots against, aim at
συμ-βουλεύω	advise
συμ-βουλεύομαι	take advice, deliberate[17]
-τῷ φίλῳ	-with a friend
*ὁ, ἡ βοῦς	ox, cow[18]
(Εὔβοια)	
*βραδύς	slow
(ἡ βραδυτής, βραδύνω)	
*βραχύς	short
(ἡ βραχύτης, βραχύνω)	
*βρέχω	moisten
*βροντή	thunder, astonishment[19]
*βροτός	mortal[20]
	Γ
*τὸ γάλα, γάλακτος	milk[1]
*γάμος	wedding, marriage
γαμέω γυναῖκα	marry a woman
γαμέομαι ἀνδρί	marry a man

16. *cp.* quivis   17. *cp. construction with* consulere
18. bos, *F* boeuf, beef; Boetia   19. bronto-saurus (σαῦρος
lizard)   20. ἄμβροτας < ἄμροτος immortal   1. (g)lac,
(g)lactis, *F* lait

γαμβρός	(a relation through marriage) brother-, sister-in-law[2]
*γάρ	for, namely, indeed
εἰ γάρ	would that
*ἡ γαστήρ, γαστρός	womb, belly[3]
*γε (encl.)	(emphasizes the preceding word; often left untranslated) at least, at any rate
γοῦν (γέ + οὖν)	1. = γε 2. (= οὖν) at any rate
*γείτων, ονος	neighbor; as adj. neighboring, akin to
(γειτονέω)	
*γελάω	laugh
(γελαστής)	
κατα-γελάω	laugh at, mock
-τοῦ ἀδελφοῦ	-one's brother
ὁ γέλως, γέλωτος	laughter
γελοῖος	amusing
*γέμω	be full
-ἐλπίδων	-of hopes
*τὸ γέρας, γέρως	gift of honor, prize, privilege
γέρων, οντος	old; old man (an elder)
γερουσίᾱ	senate, council of elders
γεραιός	old, venerable
τὸ γῆρας, ως	old age
γηράσκω	grow old
*γεύω	give one a taste of a thing (med. taste)[4]
-αἵματος	-of blood
*γέφῡρα	bridge
(γεφῡρόω)	
*γῆ (γαῖα)	earth, land[5]
γεωργός	farmer[6]
(γεωργίᾱ, γεωργέω)	
*γίγᾱς, αντος	giant

---

2. gener < gemer; γαμβρός < γαμρός; see p. 35 n. 20
3. gastric   4. gustare, F goûter, disgust   5. geology, et al.   6. < γη-ϜΟΡΓΟΣ (ἔργον); George

*γίγνομαι	to become, happen, occur; (*with prp. or adv. of place*) come[7]
τρία ἔτη γεγονώς	three years old
γίγνομαι ἐπὶ τοῖς πολεμίοις	come under the power of my enemies
ἐγένοντο οἱ σύμπαντες	all together there were
ἐγενόμην ᾿Αθήναζε	I came to Athens
δια-γίγνομαι	go through: survive; intervene, elapse
-ἄρχων	-continue governing
παρα-γίγνομαι	arrive at, be at hand
περι-γίγνομαι	result from, overcome, be, be over, survive
-σου τάχει	-overcome you with speed
γενεά	birth, race, descent[8]
ἡ γένεσις	origin, source
γνήσιος	(belonging to the true race) legitimate, noble[9]
τὸ γένος	race, descent, gender[10]
εὐγενής (ἡ εὐγένεια)	well-born, noble
συγγενής (συγγένεια)	inborn, natural
γενναῖος	noble, genuine, thoroughbred
ἡ γενναιότης	nobility
γεννάω	beget
γονεύς	ancestor, parent
ἀπό-, ἔκ-, ἐπίγονος	descendent
πρό-γονοι	forebearers, ancestors
*γιγνώσκω	1. (get knowledge) know, perceive[11]
-ἡττημένος	-that I am beaten
	2. (have knowledge) be acquainted with
	3. (understand something) conclude

---

7. *r.* γενη-, γνη-, γεν-, γον-, γγ-; gignere; king, *G* König, *G* Kind   8. genealogy   9. gnarus, (g)nasci
10. genus   11. cognosco

ἀνα-γιγνώσκω	know further, again; read
ἀπο-γιγνώσκω	give up (an intention), acquit; despair
-τῆς δίκης	-acquit of the charge
-τοῦ μάχεσθαι	-give up the fight
κατα-γιγνώσκω	recognize, find fault; sentence, condemn
-Σωκράτους τὸν θάνατον	-Socrates to death
μετα-γιγνώσκω	change one's mind; repent
συγ-γιγνώσκω	pardon; agree with[12]
συγ-γνώμη	pardon
γνώμη	understanding, judgment; opinion, mind; purpose
ἡ γνῶσις	knowledge, acquaintance
γνωρίζω	become acquainted with, perceive; make known
γνώριμος	well-known; an acquaintance[13]
ἀμφι-γνοέω	be unsure, doubtful
ἀ-γνοέω	be ignorant, not know
ἄ-γνοια	ignorance
ἀ-γνώμων	injudicious, thoughtless
ἀ-γνωμοσύνη	lack of judgment
ἀ-γνώς, ῶτος	unknown, obscure[14]
*ἡ γλαῦξ, γλαυκός	owl
*γλυκύς	sweet, pleasant[15]
(ἡ γλυκύτης)	
*γλῶττα	tongue, language
*τὸ γόνυ, γόνατος	knee[16]
γωνίᾱ	angle, corner
τρί-γωνον	triangle[17]
*γόος	weeping
*γράφω	write, paint
γραφεύς	writer, painter
γράφομαι Σωκράτη(ν) ἀσεβείας	indict Socrates for impiety

---

12. *cp.* ignosco < ingnosco have consideration   13. gnarus
14. ignotus < ingnotus (*do not confuse with n. 12*)
15. < δλυκύς; dulcis, *F* doux   16. genu, *F* genou, knee;
genuflect   17. trigonometry

γραφή	writing, writ of indictment
τὸ γράμμα	letter; (pl.) epistle; literature (learning)[18]
γραμματεύς	scribe
(γραμματεύω)	
ἀ-γράμματος	unwritten (= ἄ-γραφος); un-lettered, uneducated
συγ-γραφεύς	author, historian
*γυμνός	naked, lightly clothed; un-armed
γυμνάζω	exercise[19]
ὁ γυμναστής	trainer
γυμνάσιον	gymnastic school; (pl.) bodily exercise
γυμνής, ῆτος	a light-armed foot-soldier
(γυμνητικός)	
*γυνή, γυναικός	woman[20]
γυναικεῖος	feminine, effeminate
ὁ γυναικών, ῶνος	the woman's part of the house
*ὁ γύψ, γῦπός	vulture

Δ

*ὁ δαίμων, ονος	deity; one's "genius," lot, fortune[1]
δαιμόνιος	godlike, wonderful; remark-able
εὐ-δαίμων	fortunate, prosperous
(εὐδαιμονίᾱ, εὐδαιμονέω)	
εὐ-δαιμονίζω	account fortunate, consider happy
-σε μοίρας	-(consider) you (happy) with respect to your fate
*δάκνω	bite
*δάκρυον	tear, drop[2]
(δακρυόεις)	
δακρύω	weep, bewail

---

18. τέχνη γραμματική grammar   19. τέχνη γυμναστική gym-
nastics   20. queen; gynecology   1. demon   2. lacrima
(F larme) < dacruma, tear

*δάκτυλος	finger, toe[3]
δακτύλιος	ring, seal-ring
*δανείζω	lend; (med.) borrow
*δαπάνη	cost, extravagance
δαπανάω	expend; spend
*δαρθάνω (usu. κατα-δ.)	sleep, fall asleep[4]
*δασμός	division, sharing of spoil, tribute
*δασύς	thick, hairy[5]
(δασύνω)	
*δέ	1. but 2. and
καὶ δέ	and also, but also
*δέδοικα, δέδια	fear, be afraid
-μὴ ἀποστῶσιν	-lest they fall away
τὸ δέος	fear
ἀ-δεής	fearless
(περιδεής)	
ἄ-δεια	fearlessness, freedom from strife
δειλός	cowardly, vile; miserable
(δειλίᾱ)	
δεινός	fearful, terrible, clever
(ἡ δεινότης)	
δεινόν ἐστι, μή	it is to be feared that
δειμαίνω	fear
*δείκνῡμι	show[6]
-ἕτοιμος ὤν	-that I am prepared
ἀπο-δείκνῡμι	show forth, make known, reveal
ἐν-, ἐπι-δείκνυμαι	inform against; display
τὸ παρά-δειγμα	example, pattern, lesson[7]
δίκη	right; law; law-suit
δίκην ἐπιτίθημι τῷ ἀδελφῷ	bring suit against one's brother
δίκην δίδωμι	suffer punishment
δικάζω	judge, decide

---

3. dactyl 4. dormio 5. densus, dense 6. dico
7. paradigm

-δίκην	-the case
δικάζομαι	plead
δικαστής	judge
(δικαστήριον)	
δίκαιος	righteous, just
-εἶ ποιεῖν	-you have a right (are bound) to do something
δικαιοσύνη	righteousness, justice
δικαιόω	make right, justify; judge, condemn
ἄ-δικος	unjust, unrighteous
(ἀδικίᾱ)	
ἀ-δικέω	do harm, wrong
-τὸν ἀδελφόν	-do one's brother harm
-πολέμου ἄρχων	-unjustly begin a war
ἀδικοῦμαι	be wronged, harmed
*δείλη	afternoon
*δεῖπνον	meal, dinner (the chief meal)
(ἄ-δειπνος)	
δειπνέω	dine
*δεκάτη	the tenth part, tithe
*δέμω	build
δόμος	house[8]
δεσπότης	lord of the house, master[9]
(δεσποτέω, δεσποτίσκος, δεσποτικός)	
δέσποινα	mistress, lady
*δένδρον	tree
(δενδρήεις)	
*δεξιός and δεξιτερός	on the right hand or side, right; fortunate[10]
ἡ δεξιά	right hand
*δέρω	flay, skin; mistreat
τὸ δέρμα and ἡ δορά	skin, hide, leather[11]
(δερμάτινος)	
*δεῦρο	hither

---

8. domus; G Dom   9. despot   10. dexter, dexterous
11. epidermis

δεῦρ' εἰπέ	now then, say
*δέχομαι	take, receive
δια-δέχομαι	take over, succeed to[12]
(διαδοχή)	
προσ-δοκάω	expect, await
(προσδοκία)	
*I. δέω	bind
δεσμός	band, fetter
δεσμεύω	fetter
δεσμώτης	in chains, prisoner
(δεσμωτήριον)	
διά-δημα	headband, diadem
ὑπό-δημα	sandal
*II. δέω	need, lack
-πολλοῦ λέγειν	-be far from speaking
-τοσούτου ὑμᾶς ἐπαινεῖν, ὥστε πάνυ μέμφομαι	-I am so far from praising you that I must utterly blame you
ὀλίγου ἐδέησαν φυγεῖν	they almost fled
δεῖ	it is necessary, one must
-μοί τινος	-I have need of something
ὀλίγου δεῖν ἔφυγον	they almost fled
δέον	it being needful
τὸ δέον	that which is necessary
τὰ δέοντα	duty
δέομαι	need, have need, want, ask
-ταῦτά σου	-ask this of you
ἐν-δεής	needy, weak, lacking
(ἡ ἔνδεια)	
δεύτερος	second
-οὐδενός	-to none
*δή	1. already, now
νῦν δή	even now
	2. thus, henceforth
καὶ δὴ καί	and what is more
	3. indeed, surely

---

12. Diadochi

λέγε δή	so speak
ἄγε δή	come now
πῶς δή;	just how?
δῆτα	certainly, to be sure
δήπου	it may be, perhaps
ἤδη	already; just now[13]
*δῆλος	manifest, clear
-ἦν οἰόμενος	-he apparently thought
δῆλον ὅτι *and* δηλονότι	it is evident that
ἄ-δηλος	unclear, unknown
δηλόω	make manifest, show
-σε κακὸν ὄντα	-that you are evil
*δῆμος	country district; people, popular party
δημόσιος	public, belonging to the people *or* state
δημοσίᾳ	in the name of the people *or* state, at public expense
δημ-αγωγός (δημαγωγέω, δημαγωγίᾱ)	popular leader[14]
δημ-ηγόρος (δημηγορέω)	public speaker[15]
δημι-ουργός	(working for the people) artisan[16]
δημο-κρατίᾱ	popular government, democracy
ἀπο-δημέω	be in a foreign country, away from home, travelling
ἔν-δημος (ἐνδημέω)	native, endemic, of one's home *or* state
ἐπι-δημέω	remain at home, stay where one is[17]
παν-δημεί	with all the people, en masse
*δηόω	slay, ravage
*διά	1. (*gen.*) through,[18] while, by means of

---

13. ἤ-δή   14. demagogue (ἄγω)   15. ἀγορεύω   16. ἔργον
17. epidemic   18. dis-

-τῶν ὀρῶν	-through the mountains
-τῆς νυκτός	-during the night
δι' ἀγγέλου	by messenger
	2. (acc.) because of, for the sake of
διὰ τοῦτο	on account of this
διὰ τί;	why?
*δίαιτα	way of living, life; dwelling[19]
διατάομαι	live, stay
*διᾱκονος	servant[20]
(διᾱκονέω, διᾱκονίᾱ	
*διδάσκω	teach[21]
(διδαχή)	
διδάσκαλος	teacher
(διδασκαλεῖον)	
*δίδωμι	give[22]
ἡ δόσις	gift, giving; dose
ἀπο-δίδωμι	give back, render, yield
(ἡ ἀπόδοσις)	
ἀπο-δίδομαι	(give away from oneself) sell
ἐκ-δίδωμι	give up, give out, surrender
μετα-δίδωμι	give a share, give part of
-τῆς ἀρχῆς	-one's authority
παρα-δίδωμι	hand down, hand over
(ἡ παράδοσις)	
προ-δίδωμι	forsake, betray[23]
(προδότης, προδοσίᾱ)	
δῶρον and δωρεά	gift[24]
δωρέομαι	give a gift
δωρο-δοκέω	accept as a gift,[25] take as a bribe
*δῖος	godlike, noble, excellent[26]
εὐ-δίᾱ	fair weather
*διότι	1. wherefore 2. because

---

19. diet   20. deacon   21. doceo; disco < di-dc-sco, didactic   22. r. dō-, də (Latin dă-) dōnum, dōs, dăre; anecdote (ἀνέκδοτον)   23. prōdere, prōditor?   24. Theodore, Dorothy, etc.   25. δέχομαι   26. divus

*διπλοῦς	double, twofold[27]
(διπλόω)	
*δίσκος	round plate, discus
*δίχα	in two, apart
*δίψα	thirst
δίψω *from* διψήω	thirst
*διώκω	pursue; prosecute
-σε δειλίας	-you for cowardice
ἡ δίωξις	pursuit, suit
*δοκέω	seem, appear; suppose
δοκῶ μοι	I think[28]
δοκεῖ	it seems (good)
-μοι	-it seems (good) to me
(ὡς) ἐμοὶ δοκεῖν	as it seems to me
δέδοκται	it has been concluded
δεδογμένον, δόξαν	concluded
τὰ δεδογμένα *and* τὸ δόγμα	conclusion, opinion[29]
δόκιμος	proven, worthy
δοκιμάζω	examine, prove, test
δοκιμασίᾱ	test, examination
δόξα	1. opinion 2. honor, glory
δοξάζω	think, hold an opinion
(τὸ δόξασμα)	
ἔν-δοξος, εὔ-δ. *and*	honored, glorious, of good
εὐ-δόκιμος	report
(ἄ-δοξος, εὐ-δοξέω, εὐ-δοξίᾱ, εὐ-δοκιμέω)	
παρά-δοξος	contrary to what is expected, strange[30]
*δόλιχος	long, wearisome
*δόλος	deceit, cunning[31]
(δολόεις)	
*δοῦλος	slave
δουλεύω	be a slave, serve
δουλείᾱ	slavery, service
(δουλόω)	

---

27. diploma 28. *cp.* mihi videor 29. dogma 30. paradox 31. dolus

*δοῦπος	any dead, heavy sound
*δράκων, οντος	dragon, snake
*δραχμή	drachma[32]
*δράω	do, accomplish
τὸ δρᾶμα	production, play
*δρόμος	running, course; race course[33]
(δρομεύς)	
*ἡ δρῦς, υός	oak, tree
*δόρυ, δόρατος	timber, wood; spear
δορυ-φόρος	spear carrier, bodyguard
*δύναμαι	be able; be worth
δυνατός	mighty, capable, possible
(ἀ-δύνατος, ἀ-δυνασίᾱ)	
ἡ δύναμις	might, power[34]
δυνάστης	lord, ruler
(δυναστεύω, δυναστείᾱ)[35]	
*δύω, *usu.* κατα-δύω	put on, sink in
ἐν-δύω αὐτὸν στολήν	dress him in a cloak
(ἀπο-δύω, ἐκ-δύω)	
δύομαι	make one's way into[36]
ἀνα-δύομαι	come up, rise
ἐν-δύομαι τὸν χιτῶνα	put on one's undergarment
δυσμαί	sundown, west[37]
ἄ-δυτον	(not to be entered) innermost sanctuary, shrine

E

*τὸ ἔαρ, ἔαρος *and* ἦρος	spring[1]
*ἐάω	permit, allow, leave alone
οὐκ ἐάω	hinder, forbid
*ἐγγυάω *(and med.)*	pledge, betroth
(ὁ ἐγγυητής)	
*ἐγγύς	near, nigh at

---

32. 100 drachmae = 1 μνᾶ   33. hippo-drome (ἵππος)
34. dynamic, dynamo, dynamite 35. dynasty   36. δύω *pf.*
δέδῠκα, δύομαι *pf.* δέδῡκα   37. *cp.* occidens   1. vēr

-τοῦ τάφου	-the grave
(ἐγγύθεν)	
*ἐγείρω	awaken, rouse
(pf.) ἐγρήγορα	be awake
*τὸ ἕδος	seat; abode; statue[2]
καθ-έζομαι	sit, be seated
καθ-ίζω	set, establish; be seated[3]
καθ-έδρᾱ	seat, stool[4]
ἐν-έδρᾱ	lying in wait; ambush
ἐν-εδρεύω	ambush
ἱδρύω	establish, encamp
*ἐθέλω and θέλω	wish, will
ἐθελοντής	willing
*τὸ ἔθνος	tribe, nation
(ἐθνικός)	
*τὸ ἔθος	custom, usage, manner[5]
ἐθίζω	accustom, use
εἴωθα	be accustomed[6]
τὸ ἦθος	habit, character[7]
εὐ-ήθης	well-disposed; simple-minded
(ἡ εὐήθεια)	
συν-ήθης	familiar, of like habits
(ἡ συνήθεια)	
*εἰ	1. if 2. whether
εἰ...ἤ	whether...or
εἴθε	would that
εἴπερ	if indeed
εἴτε...εἴτε	either...or if it be this...or that[8]
ἐάν, ἄν, ἤν	1. if 2. whether[9]
ἐάν τε...ἐάν τε	if it be this...or that
*I. εἴκω	submit, obey
*II. εἴκω,	
(pf.) ἔοικα	be like, resemble, seem

---

2. sella (< sedla), sedes   3. ἴζω like sīdo < si-sd-o
4. cathedral (seat of the Bishop)   5. σϝεθ-; cp. as-suē-
tus   6. < σέ-σϝωθ-α   7. ethic   8. sive...sive   9. < εἰ
+ ἄν

ἔοικεν	it appears
ἐοικώς *and* εἰκώς	similar, like
τὸ εἰκός, εἰκότος	what is likely, probable
εἰκός ἐστιν	it is reasonable
εἰκότως	in all likelihood
εἰκῇ	without plan, rashly
ἐπι-εικής	reasonable, fitting, meet
ἐπι-εικῶς	fairly, reasonably
αἴκεια *and* αἰκίᾱ	outrage, affront[10]
εἰκάζω	make like to; liken, compare
ὡς εἰκάσαι	presumably
ἡ εἰκών, όνος	likeness; image[11]
*εἵλως, ωτος	helot, serf
*εἰμί	be[12]
ἔστι	there is, exists
ἔστι θεός	God exists
ἔστι, ἔν-, ἔξ-, πάρεστι	it is possible, permitted
οὐκ ἔστιν ὅπως	in no case whatsoever
εἶεν	good, well
ὄν, ἐξόν, παρόν	(it being) possible
τῷ ὄντι *and* ὄντως	really, actually
τὸ νῦν εἶναι	for the present
ἑκών, ἑκόντες εἶναι	willing
τὸ ἐπ᾽ ἐμοὶ εἶναι	as far as I am concerned
τὸ κατὰ τοῦτον εἶναι	as for this
οὐσίᾱ	being; essence, substance
ἐξ-ουσίᾱ	power, authority
ἄπ-ειμι	be away, distant, absent
μέτ-εστί μοι	have a part in
-τούτου	-this
πάρ-ειμι	be near, present
παρ-ουσία	a being present, presence
περί-ειμι	be around; surpass
-τοῦ φίλου σοφίᾳ	-surpass one's friend in wisdom

---

10. < ἀ-είκεια   11. icon   12. < ἐσ-μι, *cp.* es-se, ἐστίν *and* est

περι-ουσίᾱ	overabundance; surplus
σύν-ειμι	be united with, support
-τοῖς φίλοις	-one's friends
συν-ουσίᾱ	intercourse, society
*εἶμι	go[13]
πάρ-ειμι	go by, pass by; enter; come
σύν-ειμι	go with, come together, accompany
*εἴργω	shut in, shut out, hinder
-σε τῶν ἱερῶν	-bar you from the sacrifices
-μὴ ἀποκτείνειν	-forbid to kill
*εἰρήνη	peace,[14] treaty
*εἴσω and ἔσω	within, inside
(ἔσωθεν)	
*εἶτα and ἔπειτα	then, thereupon, thereafter
*ἐκ, ἐξ	from, out of, owing to[15]
ἐκ παίδων	from childhood onwards
ἐκ δὲ τούτου	thereupon, therefore
ἐκτός	without, outside, out of, beyond
-τούτων	-with the exception of these
ἔξω	outside, beyond
(ἔξωθεν)	
*ἑκάς	distant, far off, far from
-τῆς γῆς	-the earth
ἕκαστος	each, each one, every, every one
ἑκάστοτε	each time, every time
ἑκάτερος	each of two
ἑκατέρω-θεν	from each side
(ἑκατέρωθι, ἑκατέρωσε)	
*ἐκεῖ	there
(ἐκεῖθεν, ἐκεῖσε)	
ἐκεῖνος	that, that one
*ἑκούσιος and ἑκών, όντος	of one's own free will, voluntary

---

13. eo, īre   14. Irene   15. ex

ἀκούσιος, ἄκων	unwilling, involuntary[16]
ἕνεκα, ἕνεκεν	for the sake of[17]
ὑγιείας ἕνεκα	for the sake of health
οὕνεκα	wherefore; that (= ὅτι); on account of (= ἕνεκα)[18]
*ἐλαία and ἐλάā	olive tree, olive[19]
ἔλαιον	(olive) oil[20]
*ἐλαύνω	(tr.) drive, (itr.) march[21]
ἡ ἔλασις	march, expedition
*ἔλαφος	deer[22]
*ἐλαφρός	light, quick
*ἔλεγος	lament
ἐλεγεῖον	the elegiac meter (ἡ ἐλεγείᾱ)[23]
*ἐλέγχω and ἐξ-	disgrace; refute, examine; prove
ἐλέγχομαι ποιῶν	it is attested that I do
ὁ ἔλεγχος	inquiry, demonstration, refutation
*ἔλεος	compassion[24]
ἐλεέω	have compassion, pity[25]
-τὸν ἀδελφόν	-one's brother
*ἐλεύθερος	free[26]
ἐλευθερίᾱ	freedom
ἐλευθερόω	liberate
-σε κακῶν	-you from misery
(ἡ ἐλευθέρωσις)	
ἐλευθέριος	generous, liberal[27]
*ὁ ἐλέφᾱς, αντος	elephant, ivory[28]
*ἕλκω and ἑλκύω	draw, drag
(ἡ ἕλξις)	
ἡ ὁλκάς, άδος	a ship which is towed, trading vessel
*ἡ ἐλπίς, ίδος	hope, expectation
ἐλπίζω	hope, expect

16. < ἀ-ϝέκων   17. < ἐν-ϝεκα   18. < οὗ ἕνεκα   19. olīva 20. oleum, F huile, G Öl   21. cp. ἄγω also itr.   22. al- cēs, cp. elk, G Elch   23. elegy   24. later ἐλεημοσύνη > alms   25. Kyrie eleison   26. liber; libet, lubet 27. cp. liber and liberalis   28. foreign word in Greek

εὔ-ελπις	of good hope
*ἐν	in; at, on, during[29]
ἐν ᾧ (χρόνῳ)	while
εἰς, ἐς	into, within[30]
ἔνδον	inside[31]
(ἔνδοθεν)	
ἐντός	within[32]
-τῶν ὅρων	-the borders
ἔνθα	here, there; (rel.) where
(ἐνθάδε)	
ἐνταῦθα	here, there; thereupon
ἐντεῦθεν	thence, hence
*ἐνιαυτός	year
*ἔνιοι	some
ἐνίοτε	sometimes
*ἔννῡμι, ἀμφι-ἕννῡμι	dress, attire[33]
ἕννῡμαι	dress (itr.)
ἡ ἐσθής, ῆτος	clothing
ἱμάτιον	cloak, garment[34]
*ἐξαίφνης and ἐξαπίνης	suddenly
*ἐξετάζω	test, scrutinize
(ἡ ἐξέτασις)	
*ἐορτή	festival
ἑορτάζω	celebrate a festival
*ἐπεί	1. when, after that[35]
	2. (in main clause) for, since
ἐπεὶ ὅρα	behold
*ἐπ-είγω	press upon, drive forward
ἐπ-είγομαι	hasten, urge on
*ἐπί	1. (gen.) upon
	2. (dat.) on, upon, at
	3. (acc.) against, upon
ἐφ᾽ ἡμῶν	in our day

---

29. *Latin* in   30. < ἐνς   31. < ἐν-δομ (domus)
32. intus   33. < ϝεσ-νυμι, vestio (F vêtir)   34. *diminutive of* τὸ εἶμα clothing   35. *somewhat similar is* cum *with subjunctive*

ἐπὶ τούτῳ	(thereupon) on condition that; in addition to this
ἐφ᾽ ᾧ (*with inf.*)	on condition, that
ἐπὶ τοῦτο	for this purpose
*ἐπί-κουρος	helping; a helper, ally[36]
(ἐπικουρέω, ἐπικουρίᾱ)	
*ἐπιτήδειος	useful, serviceable, necessary[37]
*τὰ ἐπιτήδεια	(that which is necessary) provisions
ἐπιτηδεύω	pursue, practice
*ἕπομαι	follow[38]
*τὸ ἔπος	word, story; (*in pl.*:) epic poetry[39]
ὡς ἔπος εἰπεῖν	so to speak, almost
*ἐράω	love, desire passionately
-τῶν καλῶν	-long for the beautiful
(ὁ ἐραστής)	
ὁ ἔρως, ωτος	love, desire for
*ἔργον	work, deed
λόγῳ μέν...ἔργῳ δέ	in word...in deed
ἐργάζομαι	work, finish
(ὁ ἐργάτης)	
κατ-εργάζομαι	accomplish
ἀργός	lazy; idle[40]
(ἀργέω, ἀργίᾱ)	
ἐν-εργός	busy, active[41]
ἡ ἐν-έργεια	action, power
ὑπ-ουργός	rendering service, servant
(ὑπουγέω)	
εὐ-εργέτης	benefactor
εὐ-εργετέω	benefit
-ἕκαστον	-each one
εὐ-εργεσίᾱ	benefit

---

36. < κορσος *to* curro (< curso)   37. *cp.* necessarius
38. sequor (*F* suivre, sue)   39. Ϝέπος (εἶπον < ἔϝεπον), vox   40. < ἀ-Ϝεργός   41. energy

παν-οῦργος	(ready for anything) knave; clever, cunning[42]
ὄργανον	engine, tool, instrument[43]
*ἐρέττω	row; ply, urge
(ὁ ἐρέ-της)	
ὑπ-ηρέτης	rower; laborer, servant
ὑπ-ηρετέω	serve, help
ὁ ἐρετμός	oar[44]
*ἔρημος	lone, destitute, vacant[45]
-συγγενῶν	-bereft of kin
(ἐρημία)	
*ἡ Ἐρῑνύς, ύος	the Fury, an avenging deity
*ἡ ἔρις, ιδος	strife, rivalry
ερίζω	strive, rival
-σοι ἀνδρείᾱν	-contest your manliness
*ὁ ἑρμηνεύς	interpreter
Ἐρμῆς, οῦ	Hermes
Ἐρμαῖ	(orig. pillars with the head of Hermes) herms
ἕρμαιον	godsend, windfall
*ἕρπω and ἑρπύζω	creep[46]
*ἐρυθρός	red[47]
*ἐρῡ́κω	hold back, ward off[48]
τὸ ἔρυμα	fence, safeguard, bulwark
ἐρυμνός	fenced, fortified
*ἔρχομαι	come, go
-εἰς λόγους ὑμῖν	-come to consult with you
ἐπ-αν-έρχομαι	return
δι-έρχομαι	discuss
παρ-έρχομαι	go by, past
*ἐρωτάω	ask
-σε τοῦτο	-question you about this
ἐρωτῶμαι τοῦτο	be questioned about this
(τὸ ἐρώτημα, ἡ ἐρώτησις)	

---

42. cp. κακοῦργος criminal   43. organ   44. remus
45. rarus, hermit   46. serpo; serpent   47. ruber
48. = Hom. ἐρύομαι defend

54

*ἐσθίω	eat[49]
ἐδωδή	food, nourishment
ὁ ὀδών (ὁ ὀδούς), ὄντος	tooth[50]
*ἐσθλός	noble
*ἑσπέρᾱ	evening, west[51]
*ἔστε	until, so long
*ἑστίᾱ	hearth, domestic altar[52]
ἑστιάω	receive into one's home, feast
*ἔσχατος	furthest, last
*ἑταῖρος	companion, friend
ἑταιρίᾱ and ἑταιρείᾱ	political club
*ὁ ἕτερος	the other, one of two[53]
ἑτέρωθι	upon the other side
(ἑτέρωθεν, ἑτέρωσε)	
οὐδέτερος	neither of two[54]
(οὐδετέρωσε)	
*ἔτι	still, yet, as yet[55]
οὐκέτι, μηκέτι	no longer, no more
*ἕτοιμος (ἑτοῖμος)	ready, prepared
*τὸ ἔτος	year[56]
*εὖ	well, good
*εὕδω usu. καθεύδω	sleep; rest
*εὐθύς	straight, direct
τὴν εὐθεῖαν ὁδόν	the straight road
εὐθύ(ς) and εὐθέως	straightaway, at once
εὐθὺς νέος ὤν	from childhood on
εὐθὺ τῆς πόλεως	straight towards the city
εὐθύνω	make straight, direct
εὔθῦνα and εὐθύνη	a reckoning, an examination of accounts
*εὐνή	lair, bed
*εὑρίσκω	find, discover
τὸ εὕρημα	discovery

---

49. < ἐδ-θίω, cp. ἔδομαι; ĕdo   50. namely one who eats;
likewise dens (archaic ptc.) F dent, tooth   51. vesper,
vespers   52. vesta   53. cp. alter   54. cp. neuter
55. et   56. < Fέτος; cp. vetus

*τὸ εὖρος	breadth, width
εὐρύς	broad, wide
*εὔχομαι	vow, pray, wish[57]
-τοῖς θεοῖς	-to the gods
εὐχή	vow, prayer, wish
*τὸ ἔχθος *and* ἡ ἔχθρα	hate, enmity
ἐχθρός	hated, hateful; enemy
ἀπ-εχθάνομαι	be an enemy; be hated
ἐχθαίρω	hate
*ἔχω (ἴσχω)	have, hold[58]
ἔχων τριήρεις	-with triremes
οὐδὲν ἔχω εἰπεῖν	have nothing to say = can say nothing
ἔχω (*with inf. or indirect question*)	be able; know
εὖ (κακῶς) ἔχω	go well (poorly)
οὕτως ἐχόντων	under these circumstances
ἔχομαι πέτρας	cling to the rocks
ἐχόμενος	clinging to, holding oneself to
ἐξῆς *and* ἐφ-εξῆς	in order; next
ἡ ἕξις	a permanent condition *or* habit
ἐχυρός, ὀχυρός	firm, secure
ἀν-έχομαι	hold out, endure
-ὁρῶν	-observe with patience
ἀντ-έχω	hold out against; (*itr.*) hold out, suffice
ἀπ-έχω	hold away, be away
-τῶν ἐσχάτων	-be far from the end
ἀπ-έχομαι	abstain from
ἐπ-έχω	hold to; (*itr.*) wait, stop
ἐπ-οχή	cessation[59]
κατ-έχω	hold back, restrain; occupy, possess
μετ-έχω	partake of, have a share in

57. *with root vowel change* -o: voveo (*F* vouer, vow)
58. *r.* σεχ-, σχ-, σχη-; *for* ἴσχω *cp.* ἰσχῡρός   59. epoch

-τῶν ἱερῶν	-the sacrifices
παρ-έχω	hold ready, render; allow[60]
-ἐμαυτὸν εὐπειθῆ	-myself obedient
προ-, ὑπερ-έχω	exceed, surpass
-τῶν ἄλλων	-the others
προσ-έχω (τὸν νοῦν)	pay attention
συν-εχής	holding together, continuous
ὑπ-ισχνέομαι	promise
ἡ ὑπό-σχεσις	promise
πλέον ἔχω ἄλλων	have the advantage over others
πλεον-έκτης (πλεονεξίᾱ)	one who has more than his share; greedy
πλεον-εκτέω	have more, claim more, be greedy
-τῶν ἐχθρῶν	-have more than one's share of enemies
εὐ-ωχέω	treat well
σχέτλιος	(able to bear) bold, hardy, cruel
σχεδόν	(holding on to) near, nigh
-τι	-almost, more or less
σχῆμα	form, shape; mien; fashion[61]
σχολή	leisure, spare time; learned discussion; (pursuit in one's leisure time) study; school[62]
σχολῇ	leisurely, slowly
σχολαῖος	slow, leisurely
σχολάζω	have leisure; linger
ἡ ἰσχΰς, ύος	strength, power
ἰσχΰω	be strong, mighty
ἰσχῡρός	strong
*ἕως	while, until
*ἡ ἕως, ἕω (dat. ἕῳ, acc. ἕω)	early morning; east[63]
αὔριον	tomorrow

---

60. *cp.* praebeo < prae-habeo   61. schema   62. schola
63. aurora

Z

*ζεύγνῡμι	bridge, bind, yoke together; subjugate[1]
τὸ ζεῦγος	yoke, bridge, cart
τὸ ζεῦγμα	bond
ζυγόν	yoke, bridge[2]
ἀνα-ζεύγνῡμι	yoke *or* harness again; march off
ὑπο-ζύγιον	beast of burden[3]
*ζῆλος	zeal, jealousy, emulation
ζηλόω	rival, emulate, strive after; commend
-τὸν ἐσθλόν	-be zealous for nobility
-σε τῆς νίκης	-commend you for the victory
*ζημίᾱ	loss; penalty
ζημιόω	cause loss to one, do one damage
*ζητέω	seek, seek after, investigate
(ἡ ζήτησις, ὁ ζητητής)	
*ζῶ < ζήω	live
ζωή	life, subsistence
ζῷον	living thing, animal[4]
ζω-γράφος	painter[5]
ζωγρέω	capture alive; restore to life[6]
*ζώννῡμι	gird
ἡ ζώνη	girdle[7]
ὁ ζωστήρ, ῆρος	the warrior's belt; any belt *or* girdle

H

*ἤ	1. or; (*in a question*) whether; 2. than (*after comp.*)
ἄλλος ἤ	someone other than

---

1. iu-n-go (*F* joindre, join)   2. iugum   3. iu(g)mentum
4. zoology   5. representational artist   6. ἀγρέω hunt
after   7. zone

58

*ἦ	1. truly
-μάλα δή	-in very truth
-που	-to be sure
	2. can it be? really?
(ἦ see rel. ὅς)	
*ἥβη	manhood, youth; freshness, vigor
ἡβάω	be in the prime of youth; be young, vigorous
ἡβάσκω	come to man's estate
ἔφηβος	come of age, a young man, ephebe
*ἡγέομαι	1. lead
-τοῖς ὁπλίταις	-show the hoplites the way
-τοῦ δεξιοῦ κέρως	-command the right wing
	2. suppose, believe, hold[1]
-θεούς	-believe in the gods
-σε φίλον	-hold you to be a friend
ἡγεμών, όνος	leader
(ἡγεμονεύω, ἡγεμονικός)	
ἡγεμονίᾱ	leading the way,[2] sovereignty
δι-ηγέομαι	set out in detail; describe, narrate
(ἡ διήγησις)	
ἐξ-ηγέομαι	be leader of, direct, go first, guide
*ἥδομαι	be pleased
-(ἐπὶ) τούτοις	-about these things
-ὁρῶν	-to see
ἡδονή	pleasure, enjoyment
ἡδύς	pleasant, sweet[3]
ἀνδάνω	please, delight
(ἡδῡνω)	
ἀ-ηδής	unfriendly, unpleasant
ἄσμενος	well-pleased, glad
αὐθ-άδης	willful, stubborn
(ἡ αὐθάδεια)	

---

1. cp. duco te victorem 2. hegemony 3. < σϜᾱδύς; suāvis, suādeo

*ἥκω	have come, be here; come
καθ-ήκω	come *or* go down; extend to
καθήκει	it is meet, proper, one's duty
τὸ καθῆκον	one's duty, what is proper
προσ-ήκει	it belongs to, befits
προσ-ήκων	belonging to, befitting
*ἧλιξ *and* ἡλικιώτης	of the same age; a fellow, comrade
ἡλικίᾱ	time of life, age; manhood
πηλίκος;	how old, great?
τηλικοῦτος, τηλικόσδε	so old, so great
*ἥλιος	sun[4]
*ἧμαι, κάθ-ημαι	sit; tarry
*ἡμέρᾱ	day
ἡμερεύω	pass the day; live
τήμερον	today
μεσ-ημβρίᾱ	midday, south[5]
ἥμερος	tame; civilized
(ἡμερόω, ἡμερότης)	
*ἡμί	I say[6]
ἦν δ' ἐγώ	I said
ἦ δ' ὅς	he said
*ἥμισυς	half[7]
τῶν ἱππέων οἱ ἡμίσεις	half the riders
*ἡνίκα	when
*τὸ ἧπαρ, ατος	liver, heart[8]
*ἡ ἤπειρος	the mainland[9]
ἠπειρώτης	mainlander
ἥρως, ωος	hero, demigod
*ἥσυχος	still, quiet; gentle
ἡσυχίᾱ	stillness
ἡσυχάζω	be still
*ἥττων	weaker, inferior

---

4. < σᾱϝέλιος, sōl; helium; *F* soleil   5. < μεσ-ημρίᾱ; *cp.* meridies < medi-dies *and see* p. *35 n. 20*   6. aio
7. sēmi-   8. iecur, iecoris (*or* iecinoris)   9. Epirus

ἤκιστα	least
ἡττάομαι	be weaker, inferior
-γυναικός	-than a woman
ἧττα	defeat, discomfiture
*ἡ ἠχώ, οῦς	echo[10]

Θ

*θάλαμος	inner room; bedchamber
*ἡ θάλαττα	sea
*θάλλω	bloom, flourish
*τὸ θάλπος	warmth, heat
*θάπτω	inter, bury[1]
ὁ τάφος	grave
ταφή	burial
(ἄ-ταφος)	
ἡ τάφρος	ditch, trench
*τὸ θάρσος, θάρρος, θράσος	courage, audacity, confidence
θαρσέω	be courageous, confident, presumptuous
θαρσαλέος	courageous, encouraging, confident
θρασύς	bold, audacious[2]
(θρασύνω, ἡ θρασύτης)	
*τὸ θαῦμα	wonder, marvel, astonishment
θαυμάζω	wonder, admire, be astonished
-αὐτοῦ τοῦτο	-admire this in him
θαυμάσιος and θαυμαστός	wonderful, wondrous
*ἡ θέᾱ and τὸ θέᾱμα	view; spectacle[3]
θεάομαι	view, watch
θέᾱτρον	theater; (collectively) the spectators
θεωρός	spectator; ambassador
θεωρέω	be a spectator, behold; contemplate, consider
θεωρίᾱ	an observing; consideration; theory

---

10. echo; κατ-ηχέω resound, teach: catechumen, catechism
1. < θάφ-ιω   2. cp. audax   3. perhaps from θᾱϝᾱ > θαῦμα

*θεός, ἡ θεός, θεά	god, goddess[4]
θεῖος	godlike
ἄ-θεος	godless[5]
ἔν-θεος	full of the god, inspired[6]
ἐν-θουσιάζω	be inspired
*θεραπεύω	serve, worship; tend, heal
(ὁ θεραπευτής)	
θεραπείᾱ	service, worship; attention, healing
θεράπων, οντος	attendant, servant (f. θεράπαινα)
*τὸ θέρος	(warm time of year) summer
θερίζω	mow, harvest
θερμός	warm[7]
*θέω	run
*θῆλυς	feminine, effeminate[8]
*ὁ θήρ, θηρός and τὸ θηρίον	wild animal[9]
(θηριώδης)	
θήρᾱ	hunt, quarry, pursuit, booty
θηράω and θηρεύω	hunt, catch
(ὁ θηρευτής)	
*θησαυρός	treasure house, treasure[10]
*θνήσκω, ἀπο-θνήσκω	die, be killed[11]
τεθνάναι	be dead, dying
θνητός	mortal
θάνατος	death
(θανατόω)	
ἀ-θάνατος	immortal
(ἀθανασίᾱ)	
*θόρυβος	tumult, applause
θορυβέω	disturb, applaud
*θρῆνος	dirge, lament
θρηνέω	lament

---

4. theology, pantheon, *etc.*   5. atheist   6. enthusiasm
7. αἱ Θερμοπύλαι (Thermopylae), thermae warm baths; thermometer   8. fē-mina   9. ferus   10. thesaurus   11. *r.* θαν(α)-, θνη-, θνα-

*ἡ θρίξ, τριχός (τρίχινος)[12]	hair
*θρόνος	seat, throne
*θυγάτηρ, -τρός	daughter
*θῡμός	soul, heart; courage, passion, spirit, will[13]
ἄ-θῡμος	devoid of feeling, spiritless
ἀ-θῡμέω	be spiritless
ἀ-θῡμία	spiritlessness
εὔ-θῡμος (εὐθῡμέω, εὐθῡμία)	good-natured
ἐν-θῡμέομαι	take to heart, ponder
ἐπι-θῡμέω	set one's heart upon, desire eagerly
-σοφίας	-wisdom
ἐπι-θῡμία	longing, desire; lust
πρό-θῡμος	ready (willing), inclined to
προ-θῡμέομαι	be ready, desire eagerly
προ-θῡμία	readiness, eagerness
θῡμόομαι	become angry
*θύρᾱ	door, gate[14]
θύρᾱζε	to *or* outside the door; out[15]
θυρωρός	doorkeeper[16]
*θύω	offer, sacrifice[17]
θυσίᾱ	sacrifice, offering
*ὁ θώρᾱξ, ᾱκος	breastplate, armor

I

*ἴάομαι (ἡ ἴᾱσις)	heal, cure
ἰᾱτρός (ἰᾱτρεύω, ἰᾱτρικός)	healer, doctor
*ἴδιος	one's own, private
ἰδίᾳ	privately

---

12. trichinosis   13. fūmus   14. fores   15. θύρᾱς + δε
16. ὁράω   17. *perhaps from* θῡμός (fūmus, smoke)

ἰδιώτης	private, lay person[1]
*ὁ ἱδρώς, ῶτος	sweat
ἱδρόω	sweat[2]
*ἱερός	holy, sacred
-τῆς Ἀρτέμιδος	-to Artemis
ἱερόν	offering, temple
ἱερεύς; ἱέρεια	priest; priestess
ἱερεῖον	sacrificial animal
ἱερεύω	offer, sacrifice, slaughter
*ἵημι	send, let go, throw[3]
ἵεμαι	throw oneself into, hasten
ἀν-ίημι	let loose, unstring
ἀφ-ίημι	send out, set free, forgive[4]
ἀφ-ίεμαι τῆς σωτηρίας	give up the rescue
ἐξ-ίημι	send out, get rid of
ἐφ-ίημι	send to, let go
ἐφ-ίεμαι	enjoin, strive after
-τῆς ἀρχῆς	-dominion
μεθ-ίημι	let loose, abandon
παρ-ίημι	let pass, permit[5]
προ-ίημι (and med.)	throw before, deliver over, send before
συν-ίημι	perceive, understand
συν-ετός	intelligent, intelligible
σύν-εσις	understanding, insight
ὑφ-ίημι (and med.)	let go, give in, yield
*ἱκνέομαι and ἀφ-ικνέομαι	come to, arrive at, reach
ἱκέτης	suppliant
(ἱκετεύω, ἱκετεία)	
ἱκανός	sufficient, suitable, capable of
ἐφ-ικνέομαι (and ἐξ-ικνέομαι)	arrive at, attain
*ἵλεως, ἵλεων	gracious
*ὁ ἱμάς, άντος	strap, thong

---

1. idiot; *see note to* ἀσκητής   2. < ϝιδρόω; sudor, *F* sueur   3. ϝί-ϝη-μι; iacio   4. *cp.* a-mittere *etc.*
5. praetermitto

64

*ἵνα	(adv.) where; whither; (with sub.) that, in order that
*ἴον	violet[6]
(ἰοειδής)	
*ὁ, ἡ ἵππος	horse[7]
(ἱππικός)	
ἡ ἵππος (and τὸ ἱππικόν)	cavalry
ἱππεύς	rider, knight
(ἱππεύω)	
ἱππό-δρομος	hippodrome, race course
*ἰσθμός	isthmus, a narrow passage
*ἴσος	equal; fair; level[8]
(ἰσόω, ἡ ἰσότης)	
τὰ ἴσα σοι ἔχω	I have the same as you
ἴσως	equally, fairly; perhaps
*ἵστημι	make stand, stand[9]
ἵσταμαι	take one's stand, step, begin
ἔστηκα	have established, stand
ἡ στάσις, εως	insurrection, strife, rebellion[10]
στασιάζω	rebel, cause strife, make an insurrection
στασιώτης	rebellious; (also:) partisan
ἀν-ίστημι	disperse, set up, banish
ἀν-ίσταμαι	stand up
ἀνά-στασις	dispersion, banishment, rising up (resurrection)
ἀνά-στατος	driven from one's home, laid waste, ravaged
ἀφ-ίστημι	put off, make revolt, separate
ἀφ-ίσταμαι	stand apart, desert, revolt
-τῶν Περσῶν	-from the Persians
(ἡ ἀπόστασις, ὁ ἀποστάτης)[11]	
δι-ίστημι	set apart, divide, separate

---

6. viola   7. equus   8. iso-metrics, etc.   9. r. στα-, στη-; cp. si-st-o   10. < στάτις; cp. statio   11. Julian the Apostate

ἐφ-ίστημι	impose, appoint; (med.) be set over
-τῇ πόλει	-the city
ἐπι-στάτης (ἐπιστατέω)	one who stands by, a suppliant; master, overseer
καθ-ίστημι	set down, establish, put right, ordain
-Περικλέᾱ στρατηγόν	-appoint Pericles general
οἱ καθεστῶτες νόμοι	the established laws
μεθ-ίστημι	change, alter
μετά-στασις	a removal from one place to another; a changing, change
παρ-ίστημι	place over against
παρ-ίσταμαι	go beside, stand by[12]
προ-ίστημι	place before, appoint, (med.) assume the leadership
-Περικλέα τῆς πόλεως	-make Pericles leader of the city
προ-στάτης	leader, protector
συν-ίστημι	unite, combine
συν-ίσταμαι and συν-έστηκα	stand together, engage
ὑφ-ίσταμαι	stand ground; promise, submit to[13]
-κινδύνους	-dangers
ἐπίσταμαι	understand, know
-θνητὸς ὤν	-that I am mortal
-μάχεσθαι	-how to fight
ἐπιστήμη	knowledge, understanding, learning
ἐπιστήμων, ονος	wise, knowing
σταθμός	dwelling, abode; lodgings; a day's march
*ἱστός	mast; loom
ἱστίον	sail, web
*ὁ ἰχθῦς, ύος (ἰχθυόεις, ἰχθυοειδής)	fish[14]
*τὸ ἴχνος and ἰχνίον	track
ἰχνεύω	track

---

12. cp. assisto   13. cp. subsisto   14. early Christian
symbol: ΙΧΘΥΣ = Ἰησοῦς Χριστὸς Θεοῦ Υἱὸς Σωτήρ

K

*καθαρός	clean, pure[1]
(καθαρεύω)	
καθαίρω	cleanse
ἡ κάθαρσις	cleansing
*καί	1. and (et)
καί *and* καὶ ταῦτα	especially
καί...καί *and* τε...καί	both...and (also)
εὐθύς...καί	hardly...when (vix...cum)
ἤδη...καί	already...when (iam...cum)
οὔπω...καί	not yet...when (nondum...cum)
τὰ αὐτὰ καὶ ἐγώ	2. as (atque)[2] the same as I
ὁμοίως καὶ ἐγώ	just as I[3]
καὶ πάλαι	3. also (etiam) long ago
καὶ πάνυ, καὶ μάλα	exceedingly
πολλοὶ καὶ ἀγαθοί	4. (*not translated*) many brave men[4]
εἴ τις καὶ ἄλλος	if someone or other
	5. (*with ptc.*) although (*also* καίπερ)
καί(περ) οὐκ εἰδώς	although he does not (did not) know
καὶ...δὲ	and also, but also
καὶ δὴ καί	furthermore
καίτοι	and yet, although
καὶ γάρ	and indeed, for (etenim)
εἰ καί, ἐὰν καί	if also, although (quamquam)
*καινός	new, novel[5]
(καινόω, ἡ καινότης)	
*καίνω *and* κατακαίνω	kill
*καιρός	the right (*or* critical) moment *or* place; advantage, profit
ἄ-καιρος	unseasonable, untimely

---

1. *G* Ketzer   2. *cp*. eadem atque ego   3. *cp*. similiter atque ego   4. *cp*. multa et gravia vulnera   5. re-cens, recent

καίριος *and* ἐπι-καίριος	in season, happening at the right time; in the right place; opportune
*καίω	kindle, burn[6]
καῦμα	burning, heat
*κακός	evil, bad, cowardly
κακόν	evil, misfortune, harm
κακόω	treat badly, harm
κακό-νους	ill-disposed, evil-minded
κακ-οῦργος	knave[7]
κακ-ουργέω	perpetrate evil, harm
κακίᾱ	meanness, cowardice
*καλέω	call, name[8]
ὁ καλούμενος θάνατος	so-called death
κέκλημαι	name
ἡ κλῆσις	calling, vocation
ἐγ-καλέω	call in; indict, censure
τὸ ἔγ-κλημα	accusation, charge
παρα-καλέω	send for; encourage, exhort; demand
ἐκ-κλησίᾱ	assembly
*καλός	beautiful, good
ὁ καλὸς κἀγαθός	honorable man, nobleman, gentleman
καλοκἀγαθίᾱ	nobleness[9]
τὸ κάλλος	beauty[10]
(καλλῡνω)	
καλλωπίζω	(make one's face beautiful) adorn[11]
καλλωπίζομαι	pride oneself, adorn oneself, show off
*καλύπτω	cover[12]
ἀπο-, ἐκ-καλύπτω	uncover, reveal
(ἡ ἀποκάλυψις)[13]	
*κάμνω	be weary, tired; be distressed

---

6. < κάϝιω   7. ἔργον, *cp.* παν-οῦργος   8. clamo, clarus
9. *Greek cultural ideal*   10. calligraphy   11. *cp.* ὄψις
12. celare   13. apocalypse

-φέρων	-be weary of enduring
κάματος	weariness, labor
*κάμπτω	bend; bow, turn around
*ὁ κανών, όνος	rule, plumb line; standard[14]
κάνεον *and* κανοῦν	reed basket, bowl
ἡ κανη-φόρος	basket carrier[15]
*καπνός	smoke
κάπρος	wild boar[16]
*καρδίᾱ	heart[17]
*καρπός	fruit, profit[18]
καρπόομαι	show profit, reap the fruits
*κατά	1. (*gen*.) down, against
κατὰ τοῦ τείχους	down from the walls
λέγω κατὰ Φιλίππου	speak against Philip
	2. (*acc*.) during, in relation to, according to
κατ᾽ ἀρχάς	in the beginning
καθ᾽ ἡμέραν	daily, day by day
τὸ κατ᾽ ἐμέ	as far as it concerns me
κατὰ φύσιν	according to nature
καθά = καθ᾽ ἅ *and* καθάπερ	according to which, as
κάτω	under, downwards, beneath
(κάτωθεν)	
*κεῖμαι	lie; (*as pf. pass. of* τίθημι) be set down, fixed
διά-κειμαι	be disposed
σύγ-κειται	it is appointed
κοιμάω	lay, bring to a rest, lull to sleep
κοιμάομαι	lay oneself to rest, fall asleep, sleep
*κείρω	shear, cut short; ravage
*κελεύω	order, beseech, bid
τὸ κέλευ(σ)μα	order, command
παρα-κελεύομαι	exhort

---

14. canon   15. *girls, who in a festival procession carry gifts on their heads*   16. caper; *F* chèvre   17. cor (*F* coeur); cardi-ology, *etc*.   18. carpo, *G* Herbst, harvest

*κενός	empty, vain[19]
-ἐπιστήμης	-without knowledge
(ἡ κενότης, κενόω)	
*κεντέω	sting, stab
κέντρον	sting; center point[20]
*κέραμος	potter's clay, pot[21]
κεραμεύς	potter
(κεραμεύω, κεραμεία)	
*κεράννῡμι	mix
ἡ κρᾶσις	mixing
ὁ κρατήρ, ῆρος	mixing cup[22]
ἄ-κρᾱτος	unmixed
*τὸ κέρας, κέρατος *and* κέρως	horn; wing of an army[23]
*κεραυνός	thunderbolt, lightning
*τὸ κέρδος	gain, advantage
κερδαίνω	gain
κερδαλέος	gainful, with an eye to gain
*κεφαλή	head[24]
κεφάλαιον	mainpoint, summary
ἐγ-κέφαλος	brain
*κῆπος	garden
*κῆρυξ, ῡκος	herald, messenger
κηρύττω	herald, proclaim
τὸ κήρυγμα	public notice, proclamation[25]
ἀπο-κηρύττω	forbid
*κίνδῡνος	danger
(ἄ-κίνδῡνος)	
κινδῡνεύω	run a risk, hazard; (*impersonal*) it seems to, is likely
κινδῡνεύεις ἀληθῆ λέγειν	you are likely to speak the truth
ἐπι-κίνδῡνος	dangerous, endangered
*κῑνέω	set in motion, stir up, arouse[26]
(ἡ κῑνησις)	

---

19. cenotaph (τάφος)   20. center   21. ceramic; Cerameikos (*Potters' Quarter in Athens*)   22. crater (of a volcano)   23. cornu; rhino-ceros   24. gable   25. kerygma
26. cieo, cīvi, *G* Kino, *F* cinéma, cinema

ἀ-κῑνητος	unmoved, untouchable
*κλάζω	cry out, shout[27]
κλαγγή	clang, cry
*κλαίω	weep, bewail[28]
ἄ-κλαυ(σ)τος	unwept; unweeping
*κλάω	break (tr.)[29]
*κλείω	shut
ἡ κλείς, κλειδός	key[30]
*τὸ κλέος	repute, report, fame[31]
εὐ-κλεής	of good repute, noble
ἡ εὔ-κλεια	good report, fame
*κλέπτω	steal
(ὁ κλέπτης)	
κλοπή	theft, fraud
*κλῆρος	lot, allotment, inheritance[32]
κληρόω	choose by lot, allot
κληροῦχος	holding an allotment of land, settler[33]
*κλῑνω	incline, bend, prop against; (itr.) recline[34]
κλῑνη	couch
ἡ κλῖμαξ, ακος	staircase, ladder
*ἡ κνημῑς, ῑδος	leg-armor, greave
*κοῖλος	hollow[35]
*κοινός	common, public
(ἡ κοινότης)	
ἡ κοινὴ (διάλεκτος)	lingua franca[36]
κοινῇ	in common, publicly
κοινόν	state, commonweal
κοινόω	make common; make a sharer in
ἀνα-κοινόομαι	impart
-ἄλλοις	-to others

---

27. < κλάγγιω; clangor   28. < κλάϝιω   29. per-cello,
clādes   30. Doric κλᾱϝίς, clāvis, claudo   31. r. κλεϝ-,
κλυ-; Sopho-cles etc.; inclutus famous   32. clergy: vo-
cantur clerici, quia Dominus sors, id est pars clericorum
est   33. ἔχω   34. tri-clinium; clinic   35. < κόϝιλος,
cāvus, cave   36. The world-language after the time of
Alexander the Great

κοινωνός	(*adj.*) common; companion, partner
κοινωνέω	take part in, share
-τοῦ κινδύνου	-the danger
κοινωνίᾱ	communion, fellowship
*κολάζω	punish
(ἡ κόλασις)	
ἁ-κόλαστος	undisciplined, intemperate
(ἀκολασίᾱ)	
*κόλαξ, ακος	flatterer
κολακεύω	flatter
-τὴν πόλιν	-the citizenry
*κόλπος	bosom, lap; any lap *or* hollow
*κόμη	hair, leaves[37]
κομήτης	long-haired; comet
*κομίζω	care for, bring
*κόπτω	cut, slay[38]
κόπτομαι	(strike oneself in grief) grieve
*ὁ κόραξ, ακος	raven[39]
*ἡ κόρυς, υθος	helmet
κορυφή	top[40]
*κόσμος	order, ornament; universe[41]
κοσμέω	order, ornament
(ἡ κόσμησις)	
κόσμιος	orderly, well-mannered
*κοῦφος	light, nimble
κουφίζω	lighten; be light
(ἡ κούφισις)	
*κράζω	croak, cry out
*τὸ κράνος	helmet
*τὸ κράτος	strength, might
(κρατΰνω)	
κρατέω	(be strong) be lord over, vanquish

---

37. (*Latin*) coma   38. comma   39. corvus   40. coryphaeus
41. cosmetic

-τῶν ἐπιθυμιῶν	-master one's desires
-τοὺς Θρᾷκας	-vanquish the Thracians
κρατερός *and* καρτερός	strong[42]
κρείττων; κράτιστος	stronger, better; strongest, best
καρτερέω	be steadfast, patient; persevere
ά-κρατής	without strength, powerless
ἡ ά-κράτεια, ά-κρασίᾱ	incontinence
αὐτο-κράτωρ	independent; possessing full powers
ἐγ-κρατής	strong, disciplined, continent
ἐγ-κράτεια	self-control, continence
άριστο-κρατίᾱ (δημοκρατίᾱ, ὀχλοκρα- τίᾱ, πλουτο-κρατίᾱ, τῑμοκρατίᾱ) [43]	rule of the nobles, aristocracy
*κραυγή	screaming[44]
*τὸ κρέας, κρέως	flesh, meat[45]
*κρεμάννῡμι	hang
κρέμαμαι	(*pf.*) be hung, suspended
*κρήνη	well, spring
*κρῑθή (κρῐθ-ινος)	barley[46]
*κρῐνω	decide, discern, judge[47]
ἡ κρίσις	choice, decision[48]
ὁ κριτής	judge[49]
ὁ ὑπο-κριτής	actor, hypocrite
άπο-κρῐνομαι	reply to, answer
*κρούω	strike
*κρύπτω	cover, hide[50]
-σε οὐδέν	-nothing from you
κρύφα *and* κρύβδην	secretly

---

42. "hard"   43. *cp. also* άρχή; *historically, all European systems of government have had ancient precedents*   44. *perhaps from* κράζω *and* κόραξ   45. "raw," *G* roh; cruor, *F* cru   46. hordeum   47. cerno, certus, discrimen   48. crisis   49. critic (*from adj.* κριτικός critical)   50. crypt

-τῶν ᾿Αθηναίων	-without the knowledge of the Athenians
*κτάομαι	gain
κέκτημαι	(pf.) possess
ἡ κτῆσις	acquiring
τὸ κτῆμα	possession
*κτείνω, ἀπο- and κατα- κτείνω	kill
*κτίζω	found, establish
*κυβερνάω	govern, steer
κυβερνήτης	governor[51]
(κυβερνητικός)	
*κύβος	cube, square[52]
*κύκλος	circle, ring[53]
κυκλόω	encircle
(ἡ κύκλωσις)	
*κυλίνδω and κυλινδέω	roll
κύλινδρος	roll, cylinder
*τὸ κῦμα	wave[54]
*κύπελλον	goblet
*κύπτω	bend forward
*τὸ κῦρος	supreme power, validity
κῦρόω	validate, ratify
κύριος	having power; lord
ἄ-κῦρος	without authority
*κύων, κυνός	dog[55]
κυνικός	doglike; Cynic
κυν-ηγέτης	hunter[56]
(κυνηγετέω)	
*κωλύω	prevent, hinder
-σε μὴ μαθεῖν	-prevent you from learning
-σε τοῦ μαθεῖν	-hinder you from learning
*κώμη	village
κώμ-αρχος	village leader

---

51. gubernator   52. cubus, cubic   53. cycle, cyclops, cyclone, Cyclades   54. cumulus   55. canis (F chien)   56. ἡγεῖσθαι

κωμήτης	villager
*κῶμος	(Dionysiac) festival, revel
ἐγ-κωμιάζω	praise, laud
κωμ-ῳδίᾱ	comedy[57]
*κώπη	handle, oar
*κωφός	blunt; mute, deaf

Λ

*λαγχάνω	draw lots, obtain (by lot)[1]
(also with gen.) e.g. τάφου	-a grave
τὸ λάχος	lot, portion
Λάχεσις	the dispenser of lots (Lachesis);[2] lot, destiny
*ὁ λαγώς, ώ	hare
*λάλος	talkative[3]
λαλέω	prate, chatter; talk
*λαμβάνω	receive, take, seize[4]
λαβὼν στρατιώτας	with troops
λαμβάνομαι	get hold of, grasp
-σε τῆς δεξιᾶς	-you by the right hand
κατα-λαμβάνω	seize; hold down, check; catch, befall
μετα-λαμβάνω	partake of
-κινδῡνου	-danger
παρα-λαμβάνω	overtake; take to oneself
συλ-λαμβάνω	bring together, apprehend
-τὴν φωνήν	-comprehend the sound
-ὑμῖν	-assist you[5]
ὑπο-λαμβάνω	take up; take on, suspect; reply; entice
εὐ-λαβής (ἡ εὐλάβεια)	take in hand carefully; cautious; pious
εὐ-λαβέομαι	take care, watch for

---

57. cp. ἀοιδή   1. λαχ-   2. cp. Νέμεσις   3. onomato-
poetic: lallare, G "lallen" to stammer   4. r. λαβ-, ληβ-;
epilepsy, a disease which suddenly seizes one   5. συλλαβή
(syllaba) bringing together of sounds into a syllable

-διαβολάς	-beware of libels[6]
*λάμπω	shine; light up
ἡ λαμπάς, άδος	torch, light[7]
λαμπρός	brilliant, bright
(ἡ λαμπρότης, λαμπρύνω)	
*λανθάνω	escape the notice of[8]
-ὑμᾶς τὰ αὐτὰ ποιῶν	-do the same without your noticing
λάθρα	secretly, by stealth
-τῆς μητρός	-without the mother's knowledge
λήθη	forgetfulness[9]
ἐπι-λανθάνομαι	forget
-ἐμαυτοῦ	-think not of myself
ἐπι-λήσμων	forgetful
ἀ-ληθής	(without reserve) frank, true
ἀ-ληθεύω	speak the truth
ἡ ἀ-λήθεια	truth
ἀ-ληθινός	truthful, real
*λέγω	1. (*often also* συλλέγω) gather, assemble[10]
συλ-λογή *and* σύλ-λογος	gathering, assembly
κατα-λέγω	recount, recite
κατά-λογος	list; levy, conscription[11]
	2. say, name, speak
εὖ λέγω ὑμᾶς	speak well of you
ὁ λεγόμενος κύων	the so-called dog
ἡ λέξις, εως	speech, saying
ἀντι-λέγω	speak against
δια-λέγομαι	converse with
-νέοις	-young people
διά-λογος	conversation[12]
ἡ διά-λεκτος	discourse; language[13]
δια-λεκτική (τέχνη)	art of debating

---

6. *cp.* caveo calumnias   7. lamp   8. *r.* λαθ-, ληθ-; lateo
9. Lethe   10. colligo, legio   11. catalogue   12. dialogue   13. dialect

λόγος	1. word; speech, tale 2. concept, teaching 3. intellect, reason; ground[14]
λόγῳ μέν.. ἔργῳ δέ	in word...in deed
λόγον δίδωμι	account for[15]
ἄ-λογος (*opp.* εὔλογος)	irrational, groundless
ἀνά-λογος	corresponding, analogous
ἀπο-λογέομαι	defend oneself
ἀπο-λογίᾱ	defense
ὁμο-λογέω	confess, praise
(ὁμολογίᾱ)	
λογίζομαι	reckon, ponder
λογισμός	reckoning
*λείᾱ	booty
λῄζω (*and med.*)	plunder, ravage
λῃστής	robber
(λῃστεύω, λῃστείᾱ)	
*ὁ λειμών, ῶνος	meadow
*λεῖος	smooth[16]
*λείπω, ἀπο- *and* κατα-λείπω	leave, leave behind; leave off[17]
λείπομαι (*pass.*)	remain behind
-σου	-be inferior to you
ἐπι-λείπω	leave behind, fail
τὰ ἐπιτήδειά με ἐπιλείπει	I lack the necessities of life[18]
(ἡ ἐπίλειψις)	
παρα-λείπω	leave on one side, let remain
λοιπός *and* ὑπό-λοιπος	remaining
τὸ λοιπόν	the rest
*λειτουργίᾱ	service (for the state)[19]
*λεπτός	thin, fine, small[20]
(ἡ λεπτότης)	
*λευκός	white, lucid[21]
(λευκόω)	

---

14. mono-logue, logic   15. *cp*. rationem reddo   16. < λεῖϝος, lēvis   17. linguo, reliquus   18. *cp*. frumentum me deficit   19. *Christian worship*: liturgy   20. lepidus   21. lūx, lūcidus, lūna, light, F luire

*λεύω *and* κατα-λεύω	stone; stone to death
*λέων, οντος	lion[22]
*ὁ λεώς (λᾱός)	people[23]
*λήγω	cease from
-ἔριδος	-strife
*λίᾱν	too much, very much
*λίθος	stone[24]
(λίθινος, λιθίδιον)	
*ὁ λιμήν, ένος	harbor, haven
*λίμνη	(marshy) lake; sea (*Hom.*)
*λῑμός	hunger, famine
λοιμός	plague, pestilence
*λίνον	linen; flax: anything made of flax, linen cloth, net[25]
*λόγχη	lance
*λοιδορέω (*and med.*)	abuse, revile
(λοιδορίᾱ)	
*λούω	wash, bathe[26]
λουτρόν	bath
*λόφος	back of the neck, neck; crest *of a helmet*
*λόχος	ambush (men laying an ambush); company of about 100 men
λοχάω (*and med.*)	lay an ambush
λοχ-ᾱγός	company commander[27]
(λοχᾱγέω)	
*λύκος	wolf[28]
*λῡμαίνομαι	outrage, maltreat
*λύπη	pain, trouble
ἄ-λῡπος	untroubled
λῡπέω	trouble
λῡπηρός	painful, troubling
*λύρᾱ	lyre[29]

---

22. leo   23. Mene-laos, Nico-laus   24. lithography, monolith   25. līnum   26. lavo   27. ἡγέομαι   28. lupus 29. *a type of harp for solo or chorus;* lyric poetry

*λΰω	loose[30]
(ή λύσις)[31]	
λῦσι-τελής	(paying dues) profitable
λῦσι-τελέω	profit
κατα-λύω	terminate, destroy
*λώβη	contumely, indignity
λωβάομαι	insult

M

*μάκαρ *and* μακάριος	blessed, happy
μακαρίζω	esteem happy
-αὐτὸν θανάτου	-esteem him happy because of death
*μακρός	long[1]
μακράν (ὀδόν)	long, distant, wide
τὸ μῆκος	length, size
(μηκΰνω)	
*μάλα	very, exceedingly
μᾶλλον	rather, more
μᾶλλον δέ	but rather
μάλιστα	most, especially
τί μάλιστα;	namely what?
εἴκοσι μάλιστα	at most twenty
*μαλακός	soft, mild; weak
(μαλακίᾱ)	
μαλακίζομαι	be (become) soft, effeminate
*μανθάνω	learn, understand, seek to know, question
-φρονεῖν	-learn to think
-σε φρονοῦντα	-perceive that you are thinking
τὸ μάθημα	that which is learned, a lesson, knowledge[2]
ἡ μάθησις	act of learning; instruction
μαθητής	student, disciple

---

30. luo, solvo; *G* ver-lieren 31. analysis 1. macer
lean, meager 2. mathematics

ά-μαθής	not learned, ignorant
(άμαθίᾱ)	
*μάρτυς, υρος	witness[3]
(μαρτυρέω)	
μαρτύριον *and* μαρτυρίᾱ	testimony, proof[4]
μαρτύρομαι	have witness borne to one; call to witness
*ἡ μάστιξ, ῑγος	whip
(μαστῑγόω)	
*μάτην	in vain
μάταιος	foolish, idle
*μάχομαι	fight, contend in battle
-θεῷ	-with a god
μάχη	battle, fight
μάχιμος	warlike
μάχαιρα	sword, dagger
πρό-μαχος	fighting in front; champion
σύμ-μαχος	fighting along with; ally
(συμμαχέω, συμμαχίᾱ)	
*μέγας, μεγάλη, μέγα	large, great[5]
τὸ δὲ μέγιστον	that which is most important
μεγαλύνω	make great; extol, exaggerate
τὸ μέγεθος	greatness, size
μεγαλοπρεπής	magnificent, splendid[6]
*μέθη	strong drink; drunkenness
μεθύω	be intoxicated
μεθύσκω	intoxicate
*μείγνῡμι *and* μίσγω	mix[7]
ἡ μείξις	mixture
ἐπι-, προς-, συμ-μείγνῡμι	commingle, blend
*μέλᾱς, μέλαινα, μέλαν	black, dark[8]
*μέλει μοί	I am concerned with
-τοῦ πλούτου	-care for wealth
-τάδε πάντα	-care for all these things

---

3. martyrs   4. *G* Martyrium   5. magnus; megalith
6. πρέπω   7. misceo < mic-sceo   8. melancholy (*cp.* χόλος)

ἀ-μελής	careless, heedless
ἡ ἀ-μέλεια	carelessness, heedlessness
ἀ-μελέω	be careless, heedless
-ἑταίρου	-of a companion
ἐπι-μελής	caring for, anxious about
ἐπι-μέλεια	care, attention
ἐπι-μελέομαι *and* ἐπι-μέλομαι	take care of, cultivate
-τῶν ἄλλων	-the others
μετα-μέλει μοι *and* μετα-μέλομαι	I regret, I repent
μεταμέλει μοι ψευσαμένῳ	I regret having lied
μετα-μέλεια	regret, repentance
μελέτη *and* μελέτημα	care, attention, practice
μελετάω	care for; study, practice
*τὸ μέλι, μέλιτος	honey[9]
μέλιττα	bee
*μέλλω	1. be about to do, intend, design, purpose
οὔκ ἐμέλλεν ἐπανελθεῖν	he was not about to go back
	2. it is to be expected, that I
μέλλουσι συνήσειν	they will probably understand
μέλλων	future (*ptc. used as adj.*)
τὸ μέλλον (*and pl.*)	the future
*τὸ μέλος	limb; song[10]
ἐμ-μελής	(in tune) harmonious
πλημ-μελής	(out of tune) faulty, offending
*μέμφομαι	blame
μομφή	blame
*τὸ μένος	force, strength; ardor, wish; disposition[11]
δυσ-μενής	hostile
(ἡ δυσμένεια)	

---

9. mel   10. melody   11. *r*. μεν-, μνη-, μα- (< μγ-); mens, mentior

εὐ-μενής	well-disposed[12]
(ἡ εὐμένεια, εὐμενέω)	
μιμνήσκω	remind[13]
(ἀνα-, ὑπο-)	
-ὑμᾶς τὴν συμμαχίαν	-you of the alliance
μιμνήσκομαι	remind oneself, remember
μέμνημαι (pf.)	think upon, mention
-τῶν 'Αθηναίων	-the Athenians
-ἄνθρωπος ὤν	-reflect upon the fact that I am a human being
-ἄνθρωπος εἶναι	-take thought to be a human being
μνῆμα and μνημεῖον	memorial, remembrance
μνήμη and μνεία	memory, recollection
μνήμων	mindful
μνημονεύω	remember, call to mind, mention
ἀ-μνήμων	unmindful
ἀ-μνηστέω	be unmindful, forget
ἀ-μνηστία	forgetfulness[14]
μαίνομαι	rage, be mad[15]
μανία	rage, madness[16]
μάντις	seer, soothsayer
μαντεύομαι	divine, prophesy
μαντεία	prophesying
μαντεῖον and μάντευμα	oracle, oracular response, seat of an oracle
μαντική (τέχνη)	art of divination
*μένω	remain, wait; expect[17]
μόνιμος	remaining, steadfast
ἐμ-μένω	abide in, cleave to
ὑπο-μένω	stay behind; endure
*ἡ μέριμνα	care, thought
μεριμνάω	care for
*τὸ μέρος	part, share, lot; turn (one's turn will come)

---

12. Eumenides (*euphemistic name for the Furies*)
13. μιμνη-ισκω; memini, reminiscor, moneo "warn"
14. amnesty   15. Maenads   16. mania   17. maneo

τὸ σὸν μέρος	for your part
μόρος *and* μοῖρα	part, lot, fate[18]
εἵμαρται (εἵμαρτο)	it is (was) decreed by fate
εἱμαρμένη	destiny
*μέσος	between, middle[19]
μετά	with; after
-φίλων καθῆσθαι	-sitting among friends
-ὀργῆς βουλεύεσθαι	-counseling angrily
-τὴν ναυμαχίαν	-after the sea fight
μεταξύ	between
-Ἀθηνῶν καὶ Σαλαμῖνος	-Athens and Salamis
-δειπνοῦντες	-in the midst of dining
*μεστός	full
-λίθων	-of stones
(μεστόω)	
*μέταλλον	mine, quarry[20]
*μέτρον	measure[21]
(ἄμετρος, ἀμετρίᾱ)	
μέτριος	measured, moderate
(ἡ μετριότης)	
μετρέω	measure
συμ-μετρίᾱ	proportion[22]
*μέχρι(ς)	until
μέχρι πρὸς θάλατταν *and* μέχρι τῆς θαλάττης	as far as the sea
*μῆλον	apple[23]
*μήν	yea, indeed
ἦ μήν	yea verily
καὶ μήν	and yet, nay more
οὐ μὴν ἀλλά	assuredly not
μέν	(*strengthening*) certainly;[24] (*in contrasts:*) μέν...δέ on the one hand...on the other

---

18. Μοῖρα: *goddess of destiny, who parcels out good and bad fortune;* cp. δαίμων, Νέμεσις   19. medius, *F* mi-di 20. metallum, metal   21. kilometer, metric, trimeter, *etc.*; metiri, mensa   22. symmetry   23. mālum, melon (*Italian* mellone = large apple)   24. *weakened form of* μήν

πάνυ μὲν οὖν	quite certainly
οὐ μὲν δή	certainly not
μέντοι	certainly, at any rate; however
μά	(particle used in oaths)[25]
ναὶ μὰ Δία	verily, by Zeus
οὐ μὰ Δία	no, by Zeus
*ὁ μήν, μηνός	month[26]
*μηνύω	disclose, reveal, make known
*μήτηρ	mother[27]
μητρῷος	maternal
*μηχανή	machine, device[28]
μηχανάομαι	construct, devise
ἀ-μήχανος	without means, difficult, impossible
*μιαίνω	stain, dye, color
μιαρός	stained, defiled
τὸ μίασμα	stain
*μῑκρός	small, little
μῑκροῦ	almost
μικρότης	smallness; pettiness
*μῑμέομαι	mimic, copy[29]
(ἡ μῑμησις, ὁ μῑμητής)	
*μισθός	wage, reward
μισθόω	let out for hire
μισθόομαι	hire, retain
μισθο-φόρος	wage-earner
*τὸ μῖσος	hate[30]
μισέω	hate
*μνᾶ	mina[31]
μόγις and μόλις	with difficulty; hardly, scarcely
μόχθος	toil, hardship

25. < μν   26. mensis, F mois, G Monat   27. mater (F mère), G Mutter; μητρό-πολις metropolis   28. māchina, mechanic   29. mime (ὁ μῖμος), panto-mime   30. misanthrope   31. Attic weight; as a coin, 60 to a τάλαντον (see below)

μοχθέω	be weary with toil, be troubled, distressed
μοχθηρός	in sore distress, wretched
*μόνος	alone, only[32]
μόνον	only
-ού	-all but, well nigh, almost
ἡ μονάς, άδος	single
*μορφή	(beautiful) form, shape; appearance[33]
*Μοῦσα	Muse[34]
*μῦθος	word; speech; tale, myth
παρα-μῦθέομαι	counsel, encourage
*μύω	close one's eyes or lips[35]
μύστης	initiate (of a cult)[36]
τὰ μυστήρια	cultic mysteries
*μῶρος	dull, foolish
(ἡ μωρίᾱ)	

N

*ναί	yes (as answer); verily
*ἡ ναῦς, νεώς	ship[1]
ναύτης	sailor, seaman
ναυτικόν	a fleet
ναυ-ᾱγός	shipwrecked[2]
(ναυᾱγίᾱ, ναυᾱγέω)	
ναύ-αρχος	captain, admiral
(ναυαρχέω, ναυαρχίᾱ)	
ναύ-κληρος	shipowner
ναυ-μαχέω	fight at sea
(ναυμαχίᾱ)	
ναυ-πηγός	shipbuilder[3]
(ναυπηγέω)	
*νεκρός	dead; a corpse[4]

---

32. μόναχος, monk (cp. G München); μοναστήριον monastery; monarch, monopoly etc.   33. morphology   34. since Hesiod 9 Muses; music (μουσικὴ τέχνη)   35. mū-tus   36. mystic
1. nāvis, nauta, F navire   2. ἄγνυμι   3. πήγνυμι
4. neco; necro-logy

*νέμω	(from pasture land) deal out, distribute, apportion, assign
νέμομαι	possess, use; inhabit
Νέμεσις, εως	goddess of retribution[5]
νομή	pasture
(νομεύς, νομεύω)	
νόμος	(based upon one's portion) order, law
(ἄνομος, ἀνομίᾱ)	
νόμιμος	conventional; lawful[6]
νομίζω	think, consider
τὸ νόμισμα	anything established by custom; coin
νομο-θέτης	lawgiver[7]
(νομοθετέω, νομοθεσίᾱ)	
αὐτό-νομος	independent[8]
(αὐτονομίᾱ)	
παρά-νομος	contrary to law and custom; lawless, unjust
(παρανομέω, παρανομίᾱ)	
*νέος	young, new[9]
νέον and νεωστί	recently, lately
νεώτερα	revolutionary movements
νεωτερίζω	make changes, alter
νεότης, ητος	youth
νεᾱνίᾱς and νεᾱνίσκος	young man
(νεᾱνικός)	
*νευρά and νεῦρον	sinew, tendon[10]
*νεφέλη	cloud, fog[11]
*νέω	swim
*ὁ νεώς, ώ	temple[12]
*νή	yea, truly
*ἡ νῆσος	island[13]
νησιώτης	islander
χερρό-νησος and χερσό-νησος	peninsula[14]

---

5. cp. Λάχεσις   6. is nummus borrowed from this?
7. τίθημι   8. autonomy   9. νέϝος, novus   10. nervus,
nerve; neuralgia (τὸ ἄλγος)   11. nebula   12. also ναός
13. Peloponnesus   14. an island connected to the mainland
(ἡ χέρσος)

*νΐκη	victory
νῑκάω	conquer
νΐκην νικᾶν	gain the victory
*ἡ νόσος	sickness; distress
νοσέω	be sick
*νοῦς (νόος)	mind, understanding
νοέω	think
δια-νοέομαι	(go through one's mind) think over, intend
διά-νοια	intellect, thought
ἐν-νοέω	have in mind, consider, ponder
μετα-νοέω	change one's mind, repent
(ἡ μετάνοια)	
ὁμο-νοέω	(be of one mind) agree
ὁμό-νοια	agreement
ἄ-νους and ἀ-νόητος	foolish, ignorant
ἄ-νοια	foolishness, ignorance
εὔ-νους (opp. κακόνους)	well-intentioned
(ἡ εὔνοια, ἡ κακόνοια)	
παρά-νοια	madness
νου-θετέω	bring to mind, warn[15]
(ἡ νουθέτησις)	
*νύμφη	bride; nymph
*νῦν and νῦνί	now
τὸ νῦν	the present
τὸ νῦν εἶναι	for the time being
νῦν δέ	but now (after contrary to fact clauses)
νυ(ν) (encl.)	so, now
*ἡ νύξ, νυκτός	night[16]
νύκτωρ	by night
*νῶτον	the back

---

15. τίθημι   16. nox

Ξ

*ξανθός	yellow (*of various shades*)
*ξένος	foreign; foreigner; house guest; mercenary
ξένιος (*opp.* ἄ-ξενος)[1]	hospitable
ξενίᾱ	hospitality
ξενίζω	receive a guest
πρό-ξενος	state visitor
(προξενίᾱ)	
ξενικόν	mercenary army
*ξέω	scrape, carve
*ξηρός	dry, parched
(ξηραίνω)	
*τὸ ξίφος	sword
(ξιφίδιον)	
*ξύλον	wood, beam
(ξύλινος)	

Ο

*ὁ, ἡ, τό	the
	1. (*as demonstrative*:)
ὁ μέν...ὁ δέ	the one...the other
ὁ δέ	but the other
τὸ (τὰ) μέν...τὸ (τὰ) δέ	partly...partly
καὶ τὸν εἰπεῖν	and he said
πρὸ τοῦ	before, previously
ὅδε	this
ἔλεγε τάδε	he spoke as follows
ὧδε	in the following manner
τῇδε	here
τότε	then
τοτὲ μέν...τοτὲ δέ	at one time...at another
οὗτος	this
καὶ ταῦτα	and that too, and more than that

---

1. εὔξεινος πόντος the Black Sea (euphemistic)

ταύτῃ	in this way, in this respect
τοῦτο μέν...τοῦτο δέ	on the one hand...on the other (*stronger than* μέν... δέ)
	2. (*as article*:)
ὁ Μιλτιάδου	the son of Miltiades
τὰ τῆς πόλεως	the affairs of state
ὅς	he, this one (*broadening the nom.* ὁ *by adding* ς)
ἦ δ' ὅς	he said
ὥς *or* ὧς	so, thus
καὶ ὥς	even so, nevertheless
οὐδ' ὥς	not even so
ὀβολός	obol (*6 to the drachma*)
*ἡ ὁδός	road, way
ὁδεύω *and* ὁδοι-πορέω	be on the way, march, journey
εἴσ-οδοι *and* πρόσ-οδοι	approaches, entryways
κάθ-οδος	descent[1]
περί-οδος	the way around, circuit[2]
σύν-οδος	coming together, assembly[3]
*ὀδύρομαι	wail, bewail
*ὄζω	smell, have a smell[4]
-οἴνου	-of wine
ὀδμή *and* ὀσμή	smell
εὐ-ώδης	sweet smelling
ὀσφραίνομαι	smell, scent
*οἶδα (*inf.* εἰδέναι)	know[5]
-θνητὸς ὤν	-that I am mortal
-σε θνητὸν ὄντα	-that you are mortal
οἶδ' ὅτι	surely
σύνοιδα	understand; share in the knowledge
σύνοιδα ἐμαυτῷ ψευσάμενος *or* ψευσαμένῳ	I am aware that I have lied
τὸ εἶδος *and* ἡ ἰδέᾱ	form, shape; figure, idea[6]
εἴδωλον	image, idol

---

1. cathode   2. period   3. synod   4. < ὄδιω; odor, oleo, ozone, *F* odeur, odor   5. Ϝοιδ-, Ϝειδ-, Ϝιδ- (*for example, in* ἱστορίᾱ); video (*F* voir, view)   6. ideal

ἱστορέω	learn, inquire
ἱστορίᾱ	investigation; inquiry[7]
*οἶκος *and* οἰκίᾱ	house, dwelling[8]
(οἰκίδιον)	
οἴκοι	at home
(οἴκαδε, οἴκοθεν)	
οἰκεῖος	domestic; akin, intimate, one's own
οἰκέτης	house slave
οἰκέω (ἐν-)	dwell
(τὸ οἴκημα, ἡ οἴκησις)	
ἡ οἰκουμένη (γῆ)	the inhabited world[9]
οἰκίζω	build a house; found a settlement
δι-οικέω	manage a household[10]
(ἡ διοίκησις)	
ἄπ-οικος	(far from home) emigrant, colonist
ἀπ-οικίᾱ	colony
μέτ-οικος	resident alien
περί-οικος	neighboring; neighbor
οἰκο-δομέω	build (a house)[11]
οἰκο-νόμος	housekeeper, steward[12]
(οἰκονομέω, οἰκονομίᾱ, οἰκονομικός)	
*οἶκτος	pity, compassion
οἰκτρός	pitiful, pitiable
οἰκτίρω *and* οἰκτίζω	pity
*οἴμοι	woe is me!
οἰμώζω	wail, lament
(οἰμωγή)	
*οἶνος	wine[13]
*οἴομαι *and* οἶμαι	think, intend
*οἶος	of such a sort, manner *or* kind as...

---

7. *G* Historie, history 8. vīcus village; *cp*. Greenwich
etc. 9. ecumenical 10. diocese 11. δέμω 12. νέμω; economy 13. vīnum, *F* vin, *G* Wein

οἴῳ σοὶ ἀνδρί = τοιούτῳ, οἷος σὺ εἶ	a man like you
τοιοῦτος εἶ, οἷος (= ὥστε) πείθεσθαι	you are of the sort that can be persuaded

thus:

οἷός τέ εἰμι	I am able to (*with inf.*)
οἷόν τέ ἐστι	it is possible
οἷον, οἷα	as, for example
*ἡ, ὁ οἷς, οἰός	sheep[14]
*οἰστός	arrow
*οἴχομαι	have gone, be gone
ᾤχετο ἀπιών	he has up and gone
ᾤχετο ἀποπλέων	he has sailed away and gone
*οἰωνός	bird of prey, vulture
*ὄκνος	cowardice, fear
ὀκνέω	cower, fear
ὀκνηρός	cowering, hesitating
*ὄλβος	prosperity, bliss, luck
ὄλβιος	lucky, happy
*ὀλίγος	few, little
ὀλίγου	within a little, almost
οἱ ὀλίγοι	the oligarchs
ὀλιγωρέω	show little regard for
-τῶν φίλων	-one's friends
*ὄλλῡμι *and* ἀπ-όλλῡμι	destroy; lose[15]
ἀπ-όλλυμαι	perish
ὄλεθρος	ruin, destruction
ὀλέθριος	deadly
*ὅλος	whole[16]
*ὀλοφῡρομαι	wail, bewail
*ὄμβρος	rain (storm)[17]
*ὅμῑλος	mob; an assembled crowd
ὁμῑλέω	associate with
-κακοῖς	-evil men
ὁμῑλίᾱ	company, intercourse

---

14. ovis   15. ab-oleo; *cp.* perdo, pereo   16. < ὅλϜος, salvus; cat-holic   17. imber

*ὄμνῡμι	swear, invoke
-τοὺς θεούς	-the gods
*ὁμός	common, one and the same[18]
ὁμοῦ	at once, together
-τοῖς ἄλλοις	-with the others
ὁμόσε	to the same spot, in the same direction
ὁμῶς	equally, alike; together
ὅμως	nevertheless, yet
ὅμοιος and ὁμοῖος (ἀνόμοιος)	like, similar
ὁμοιόω	make like, liken
ὁμαλής and ὁμαλός (ἀνώμαλος, ἀνωμαλία)[19]	level, even
*ὀμφαλός	navel, middle point[20]
*τὸ ὄναρ, τοῦ ὀνείρατος and ὁ ὄνειρος	dream
*τὸ ὄνειδος	report; blame
ὀνειδίζω	blame; throw a reproach upon
*ὀνίνημι	profit, benefit
-τοὺς φίλους	-one's friends
ὀνίναμαι	take pleasure
-σοῦ	-in you
*τὸ ὄνομα	name; report; word, saying[21]
ὀνομάζω	name
ἀν-ώνυμος	nameless, unknown
ἐπ-ώνυμος	named after
εὐ-ώνυμος	of good name; left[22]
*ὄνος	donkey[23]
ἡμί-ονος	mule
*ὁ ὄνυξ, υχος	nail, talon, hoof[24]
*ὀξύς (ἡ ὀξύτης, ὀξύνω)	sharp, pointed; keen[25]

---

18. cp. ἅμα   19. anomaly   20. umbilīcus   21. nomen (F nom), G Name; anonymous, pseudonym, Hieronymus   22. euphemism (cp. n. to ξένος)   23. ὄνος and asinus perhaps loan-word from Asia Minor; F âne   24. unguis, F ongle, G Nagel   25. acer; oxide, oxygen

παρ-οξΰνω	sharpen, provoke
*ὄπισθε(ν)	behind; after, later
-ἐμοῦ	-behind me
ὀπισθο-φύλακες	rear guard
ὀπίσω	behind, backwards
ὀψέ	after a long time, late, too late
-τῆς ἡμέρας	-late in the day
*ὅπλον	any tool _or_ implement
(ἄνοπλος)	
τὰ ὅπλα	weapons; (army) camp
ὁπλίζω	arm; make ready
(ἡ ὅπλισις)	
ὁπλῖτης	heavily armed foot soldier, hoplite
(ὁπλῑτεύω, ὁπλῑτικός)	
ἔν-οπλος	armed
παν-οπλίᾱ	in full armor
*ὁράω	see[26]
-σε κείμενον	-you lying down
τὸ ὅραμα	view, sight; vision[27]
ἔφ-ορος	overseeing; overseer
(ἐφορεύω)	
περι-οράω	look around, overlook, suffer
-τὴν χώραν πορθουμένην	-the land to be plundered
προ-οράω	look ahead, foresee[28]
φρουρά̱	watch[29]
φρουρός	guard
(φρουρέω)	
φρουρίον	fort, lookout
φρούρ-αρχος	leader of the guard, officer
*ὀργή	anger; disposition
ὀργίζω	make angry
ὀργίζομαι	be angry
*ὀρέγω	stretch out, extend[30]

---

26. < Ϝοράω, vereor   27. pan-orama   28. _cp_. provideo
29. < προ _and_ ὁράω; _cp_. prūdens < pro-videns _in addition to_ prōvidens   30. rego

ὀρέγομαι	stretch oneself out, reach out, reach, grasp
-δόξης	-at glory
ὀργυιά	span (of the outstretched arms)
*ὀρθός	straight, right[31]
ὀρθῶς	rightly, truly
ὀρθόω	set straight; improve
(ἐπ)αν-ορθόω	set upright again
κατ-ορθόω	set upright, put right; (itr.) be successful
ὄρθιος	steep, high
*ὄρθρος	morning (twilight)
*ὄρκος	oath; alliance
ἐπί-ορκος (ἐπιορκέω, ἐπιορκίᾱ)	swearing falsely
ἐπιορκέω θεούς	bear false witness before the gods
*ὀρμή	assault, attack
ὀρμάω	urge on; (itr.) hasten
ὀρμάομαι	hasten, be eager
*ὁ ὅρμος	anchorage; a haven, refuge
ὁρμέω	lie at anchor
ὁρμίζω	bring to anchor, (med.) be at anchor (at rest)
*ὁ, ἡ ὄρνῑς, ῑθος	bird[32]
*τὸ ὄρος	mountain
*ὁ ὅρος	boundary; measure[33]
τὰ ὅρια	frontier[34]
ὁρίζω	define, divide along a boundary[35]
ὅμ-ορος	sharing the same border; neighbor
ἀ-όριστος	without boundaries, indefinite[36]
*ὀρύττω (τὸ ὄρυγμα)	dig

---

31. arduus; orthodox etc. 32. ornithology 33. cp. defini-tion 34. cp. locus: loca 35. horizon 36. aorist

94

ἡ δι-ῶρυξ, υχος	trench, canal
κατ-ορύττω	bury
*ὀρχέομαι	dance
(ὀρχηστής, -τήρ)	
ὀρχήστρᾱ	place for dancing (in the theater)[37]
*ὅς, ἥ, ὅ	(*rel.*) who, which, that
(*generalized*) ὅστις, ἥτις, ὅτι (ὅ, τι)	
εἰσὶν οἵ	there are those who; some
οὗ	where
οἷ	whither
ὅθεν	whence
ᾗ	where; how
ἀφ' οὗ, ἐξ οὗ	after which, since
ἐν ᾧ	during
ἐφ' ᾧ	on the condition that
ὅτι	that, because (*before indirect statements not translated*)[38]
οἷος	such a sort
ὅσος	so great, so wide, so much
ὅσῳ...τοσούτῳ	the (more)...(so much) the (more)
ὅσον	insofar
ὅσον εἴκοσι	about twenty
ὡς	as[39]
	(*with nouns*)
ὡς φύλαξ	as a guard
	(*with adj.*)
ὡς καλόν	how beautiful
	(*with superl.*)
ὡς τάχιστα	as quick as possible
	(*with numbers*)
ὡς ἕξ	some six

---

37. orchestra   38. *cp. the origin and meaning of the conjunctions* quod *and* that   39. *cp. the development of* ut (*also as a conjunction*)

	(*with finite verb*)
ὡς ἐπαίδευες	1. how (that, because, as) you teach
	2. if indeed you teach
	3. for you teach
ὡς τάχιστα ἐπαίδευσας	as soon as you have taught
ὡς παιδεύῃς	so you may teach
ὡς	(*with infinitive*) so that (*with ptc.: in a subjective statement*) because, as if, as I see it (*with fut. ptc.*) in order to
ὥσπερ	just as
ὥστε	1. (*in main clause*) and thus
	2. (*in subordinate clause*) so that
	3. (*with infinitive*) so that; on the ground that
*ὅσιος (ἡ ὁσιότης, ἀνόσιος)	(following divine and natural laws) pious, holy
*ὀστέον (-οῦν)	bone[40]
ὄστρακον	potsherd
ὀστρακισμός	ostracism
*οὐ (οὐκ, οὐχ, οὐχί)	I. not (*in independent clauses*)
οὐ μάλα, οὐ πάνυ	not by any means
	observe the placement of οὐ:
οὐκ εἶδον οὐδένα	I have seen no one
οὐδένα οὐκ εἶδον	there is no one I have not seen
οὐδέ	and not, also not, but not, not once
οὐδαμοῦ (οὐδαμῇ, οὐδαμόθεν)	nowhere
οὐδαμῶς	in no way
οὐδείς	no one
οὐδέν	in nothing, by no means
οὐκέτι	no longer[41]
οὔποτε	never
οὔπω	not yet[42]

---

40. ὅς   41. *cp.* non iam   42. *cp.* non dum

οὐπώποτε	at no time
οὔτε...οὔτε	neither...nor
οὔτε...τε	on the one hand not...on the other[43]
	II. (*not translated in ὡς clauses after a verb of denial*)
ἀμφισβητῶ, ὡς οὐκ ἀληθῆ λέγομεν	doubt that we speak the truth
*μή	I. not (*in dependent clauses*)[44]
μή, ἆρα μή, μῶν (= μὴ οὖν) οἴει	do you actually not believe in anything?
	II. (*not translated with the inf. after verbs of denial and hindrance, etc.*)
ἠρνοῦντο μὴ πεπτωκέναι	they denied that they had fallen
οὐκ ἠρνοῦντο μὴ οὐ πεπτωκέναι	they did not deny that they had fallen
*οὖν	then, therefore, accordingly
δ' οὖν	but surely, always
οὔκουν	(*in questions*) it is not, is it? (*in inferring*) not therefore, so not (*in confirming*) surely not
οὐκοῦν	(*with this accentuation it loses negative connotation*) therefore, then, accordingly[45]
*οὐρανός	heaven, sky
*τὸ οὖς, ὠτός	ear[46]
*ὀφείλω	owe, ought
ὤφελε ζῆν	would that he were alive; he really should be alive
ὤφελες ἐλθεῖν	you really should have come
ὀφλισκάνω	be found guilty; incur
-μωρίαν	-bring on the charge of folly
-θανάτου	-be found guilty of a capital crime

---

43. *cp.* neque-et   44. *in clauses which contain a wish, prohibition, intention, condition, or infinitive; as for* οὐ μή *and* μὴ οὐ *see your grammars*   45. = οὖν
46. auris, *F* oreille, *G* Ohr

*τὸ ὄφελος	profit
ὠφελέω	profit, help
-τοὺς φίλους	-one's friends
ἡ ὠφέλεια	profit, help
ὠφέλιμος	profitable
*ὁ ὄφις, ὄφεως	snake
*ὄχθη	hill, raised ground
*ὄχλος	crowd, mob
ἐν-οχλέω	trouble, disturb
ὀχλο-κρατίᾱ	mob rule
*ἡ ὄψις	sight, vision[47]
ὄψομαι	(*fut. of* ὁράω)
τὸ ὄμμα	sight, eye; glimpse
ὀφθαλμός	sight, eye
κάτ-οπτρον	(on which one sees) mirror[48]
ὕπ-οπτος	looking askance; suspected; suspecting
ὑπ-οπτεύω	be suspicious[49]
ὑπ-οψίᾱ	suspicion
μέτ-ωπον	forehead
πρόσ-ωπον	face, person
*ὄψον	meat; any rich fare

Π

*ὁ παιάν, ᾶνος	paean; war song, victory song[1]
παιᾱνίζω	chant the paean
*παῖς, παιδός (ὁ, ἡ) (παιδίον, παιδίσκος)	child, servant[2]
ἄ-παις	childless
παιδεύω	teach, educate
παιδείᾱ	education
παίζω	play, sport

---

47. *r.* οπ- (oqu-), oculus; optics   48. *made from polished metal*   49. *really*: take a look from below; *cp.* suspicio < sub-specio   1. *orig. a chorus to the honor of the healing god Apollo*   2. *cp. the meaning of* puer

παιδ-αγωγός	pedagogue, teacher[3]
(παιδαγωγίᾱ, παιδαγωγέω, παιδαγωγικός)	
παιδο-τρίβης	trainer, coach[4]
*παίω	slay, strike
*πάλαι	of old, formerly
παλαιός	old, ancient
τὸ παλαιόν	formerly
*πάλη	wrestling match, contest
παλαίω	wrestle, contend
(ὁ παλαιστής)	
τὸ πάλαισμα	struggle
παλαίστρᾱ	palaestra, wrestling school
ἀντί-παλος	(wrestling against) fighting against; rival, adversary
*πάλιν	again
ἔμ-παλιν and τοὔμπαλιν	backwards, back
*παρά	1. (with gen.) from
τὰ παρ᾽ ὑμῶν λεγόμενα	your words
	2. (with dat.) beside
τὰ παρὰ θαλάττῃ χωρία	the lands by the sea
	3. (with acc.) along, to; against
παρὰ τὰ ὄρη	along the mountains
ἐλθεῖν παρὰ τὸν στρατηγόν	to come to the general
παρὰ τοὺς ὅρκους	contrary to the oaths
*παράδεισος	garden, park[5]
*παρειά	cheek
*παρθένος	maiden
ὁ Παρθενών, ῶνος	Parthenon (Temple of Athena on the Acropolis)
*παροιμίᾱ	proverb
*πᾶς, πᾶσα, πᾶν	all, whole; every[6]
πάντῃ	everywhere
(πάντοσε, πάντοθεν)	

---

3. *a slave, who leads his pupil to school*   4. τρίβω
5. paradise   6. pan-orama

πάντως, πάμπαν, παντά-πασιν	wholly, completely
πάνυ	very much
παντοῖος *and* παντοδαπός	of all sorts
πανταχῇ *and* πανταχοῦ (πανταχόσε, πανταχόθεν)	everywhere
ἅ-πᾱς	all together, every
σύμ-πᾱς	all together
*πάσχω	suffer, experience[7]
τί παθὼν ποιεῖς;	how do you come to write poetry, why do you write poetry?
εὖ πάσχω	do well
τὸ πάθημα	sorrow, suffering
τὸ πάθος	sorrow, suffering; passion[8]
ἀ-παθής (ἡ ἀπάθεια)	(not suffering:) insensible, unwilling to suffer[9]
τὸ πένθος	sorrow, grief
πενθέω	wail, bewail
*πατάττω	beat, strike
*πατήρ	father[10]
πάτριος, πατρικός, πατρῷος	belonging to one's father, hereditary, patriarchal
ἡ πατρίς, ίδος	fatherland[11]
προ-πάτωρ, ορος	forefather
*παύω	make to cease, stop
-σε τῆς ἀρχῆς	-depose you from office
-σε γελῶντα	-stop you from laughing
παύομαι	rest, cease
-τῆς μάχης	-from battle
-ἐσθίων	-eating
ἀνα-παύομαι	take one's rest, sleep
*παχύς (ἡ παχύτης, παχύνω)	thick, fat[12]
*πέδον	ground, earth[13]
ἔμ-πεδος	(on the ground) steadfast, firm

7. *r.* πενθ-, πνθ- > παθ-; πάσχω < πάθ-σκω (*perhaps not related to* patior) 8. pathos, sympathetic 9. apathetic 10. pater, patronus, *F* père, *G* Vater 11. *really an adj.* πατρὶς γῆ; *cp.* patria 12. pinguis 13. *r.* πεδ-, πηδ-, ποδ-

πεδίον	plain
πεζός	on land, on foot
πεζόν	land army, foot soldiers
*ἡ τράπεζα	table[14]
*πέδη	(foot) fetter[15]
πηδάω	leap
πηδάλιον	rudder
ὁ πούς, ποδός	foot[16]
ἐκ-ποδών (= ἐκ ποδῶν)	out of the way
ἐμ-ποδών	in the way
ἐμ-ποδίζω	hinder
τρί-πους	tripod (*three-footed kettle*)
*πείθω	persuade[17]
πείθομαι (*pass.*)	obey
πέποιθα	trust
ἡ πειθώ, οῦς	persuasion
ἀνα-πείθω	persuade, seduce
ἀ-πειθής	disobedient
(ἀπειθέω, ἀπείθεια)	
πιθανός	persuasive; obedient
*ἡ πίστις	trust, faith; treaty
πίστεις ποιεῖσθαι	make a treaty
πιστός	trusty, faithful
(ἡ πιστότης)	
ἄ-πιστος	untrustworthy, unfaithful
ἀ-πιστέω	disbelieve, distrust
ἀ-πιστίᾱ	distrust, unfaithfulness
*πεινήω	hunger
*τὸ πέλαγος	sea
*πέλας	near
-τῆς μητρός	-one's mother
πελάζω	draw near, approach
πλησίος	near, neighboring
πλησίον τοῦ οἴκου	near one's house
πλησιάζω	draw near, approach

---

14. *from* τετράπεζα four-footed; trapeze   15. pedica; *thus* expedire, impedire   16. pes, *F* pédale, *G* Fuss   17. *r.* πειθ-, ποιθ; πιθ-; fīdo, fides, foedus, *F* foi, faith

παρα-πλήσιος	coming near, resembling
*πέλτη	light (leather) shield[18]
πελταστής	lightly armed soldier
*πέμπω	send
πομπή	sending; solemn procession[19]
μετα-πέμπομαι	summon, send for
*πένομαι	work (for one's living); be poor
πένης, ητος	a poor person
πενίᾱ	poverty
πόνος	task, work, labor, toil
πονέω	labor
πονηρός (ἡ πονηρίᾱ)	painful; bad, toilsome, useless
ἐπί-πονος	toilsome; laborious
*πέπλος	cloth; woman's cloak[20]
*τὸ πέρας, ατος	border, end, goal[21]
πέρᾱν	on the other side, across
περάω	drive across or through; traverse, pass over
περαιόω	carry to the opposite side, carry over or across
ἄ-πειρος	boundless, endless
περαίνω	fulfill, bring to a conclusion
ἡ πεῖρα	a try; an attempt[22]
πειράω and πειράομαι	try, attempt; have experience of
-κακῶν	-sorrow
ἔμ-πειρος	experienced
ἐμ-πειρίᾱ	experience
ἄ-πειρος	inexperienced
ἀ-πειρίᾱ	inexperience
πόρος	path, way; means[23]
ἄ-πορος	1. (without passage) impassable; difficult

---

18. pellis, pelt, F peau   19. pomp   20. cp. toga   21. per, periculum   22. experi-mentum   23. porta, portus; βόσπορος = βοὸς πόρος, cp. Oxford and Ochsenfurt am Main

ἄ-πορος	2. (without means or way) at a loss, helpless
ἀ-πορέω	(be without means or way) be at a loss, in difficulty
ἀ-πορίᾱ (εὔπορος, εὐπορέω, εὐπορίᾱ)	want of resources; difficulty
πορεύω	carry, convey (*tr.*)
πορεύομαι	travel, go, march
πορείᾱ	march
πορίζω	bring, provide
πορίζομαι	procure
πορθμός	ferry
πορθμεύς	ferryman
ἔμ-πορος	trader, merchant
ἐμ-πόριον	trading place
ἔ-πορον	bring to pass, give (*2nd aor.* *from* πόρω)
πέπρωται	it has been fated
πεπρωμένη	fate, destiny
*περί	1. (*with gen.*) over, about[24]
διαλέγεσθαι περὶ εἰρήνης	discourse on peace
περὶ ὀλίγου ἡγεῖσθαι (ποιεῖσθαι)	reckon a thing of little worth
	2. (*with dat.*) around, about; on account of
κινδῡνεύειν περὶ τῇ ψυχῇ	risk one's life
	3. (*with acc.*) around; about
περὶ τὴν πόλιν	around the city
περὶ μέσας νύκτας	about midnight
ἁμαρτάνειν περὶ τοὺς νόμους	break the law
*πέριξ	round about, all around
περιττός	overabundant, overflowing; extraordinary
*πετάννῡμι	spread[25]
*πέτομαι	fly[26]
τὸ πτερόν *and* ἡ πτέρυξ, υγος	bird

---

24. *cp.* per-magnus   25. pateo, pando, passus   26. penna < petna, feather, *G* Feder; peto, impetus

πτερόεις, πετεηνός *and* πτηνός	feathered, winged
*πέτρᾱ *and* πέτρος (πετρώδης)	rock, stone[27]
*πηγή	spring, well
*πήγνῡμι	fix, make fast[28]
πήγνυμαι	become fixed, impale
πάγος	rock; ice, frost[29]
*πηλός	clay
προ-πηλακίζω	(cover with mud) abuse, treat with indignity
*ὁ πῆχυς, εως	elbow, forearm
*πιέζω	press, squeeze, crush
*πικρός	bitter, sharp[30]
*πίμπλημι	fill[31]
-οἴνου	-with wine
πλήθω	be full
τράπεζα πλήθει κρεῶν	the table is spread with meat
πλῆθος	crowd
πλήρης *and* πλέως, ἔκ-, σύμ-πλέως (πληρόω, ἡ πλήρωσις)	full
ἄ-πληστος	(not to be filled) insatiable
*πίμπρημι	kindle, burn
*πῑ́νω	drink[32]
(ἡ πόσις, ὁ συμπότης)	
ποτόν *and* τὸ πῶμα	drink
συμ-πόσιον	drinking party, banquet
*πιπρᾱ́σκω	sell
(ἡ πρᾶσις)	
*πῑ́πτω	fall[33]
τὸ πτῶμα *and* ἡ πτῶσις	fall
ἐκ-πῑ́πτω	fall from, be banished

---

27. petr-oleum, Peter, *F* perron   28. pa-n-go, pax; fair
29. Áreopagus = Ἄρειος πάγος   30. pi-n-go, *F* peindre,
paint   31. impleo, plenus, full, *G* voll; plebes   32. *r.*
πι-, πο-, πω-; poculum, pōto (*cp.* πέπωκα); bibo < pibo,
F boire   33. *perhaps from* πέτομαι

-τῆς πόλεως	-from the city
ἐμ-, περι-πίπτω	fall upon
-κακοῖς	-bad times
τὸ σύμ-πτωμα	chance, accident[34]
*ἡ πίτυς, υος	pine tree[35]
*πλάνη	wandering, error
πλανάω	make to wander, err
πλανάομαι	wander, err
πλάνης, ητος and πλανήτης, ου	wanderer, planet[36]
*πλατύς	flat, broad, wide[37]
*πλάττω	form, mold
τὸ πλάσμα	anything molded, figure, image[38]
πλάστης (πλαστικὴ τέχνη)	sculptor, modeler[39]
*πλέκω (τὸ πλέγμα)	twist[40]
*πλευρά and πλευρόν	sides, ribs
*πλέω	sail[41]
πλοῦς	voyage
πλοῖον	ship
*πλήν	except
-τριῶν	-three
*πλήττω	strike, wound
πληγή	blow, wound[42]
πλῆκτρον	(instrument for striking:) spear-point; pick (for a lyre)
ἐκ- and κατα-πλήττω	astound, scare (tr.); (pass.) scare (itr.)
ἐκπλήττομαι τοὺς κινδύνους	shrink from the dangers
*πλοῦτος (πλουτέω)	wealth
πλούσιος	wealthy

---

34. symptom   35. pinus   36. ἀστὴρ πλανήτης planet
37. platea (G Platz)   38. blood plasma   39. plastic
40. plecto   41. r. πλεϝ-, πλοϝ-   42. pla-n-go; plague

πλουτίζω	enrich, make wealthy
πλουτο-κρατίᾱ	rule of the wealthy[43]
*πλῦνω	wash clean
*πνέω	blow, breathe[44]
τὸ πνεῦμα	breath, spirit
ὁ πνεύμων, ονος	lung[45]
ἀνα-πνέω	breathe again, have a respite
*πόθος	yearning
πόθεω	yearn after
*ποιέω	make, do
-εὖ τοὺς φίλους	-well by one's friends
τὸ ποίημα	(that which is made) a work; poem
ποίησις	a making: forming, creating; poetry
ποιητής	creator, poet[46]
ἀντι-ποιέομαι	lay claim to, contend with
-παιδείας	-apply oneself to one's education
-τῆς ἀρχῆς τῷ δεσπότῃ	-contest with the despot for the rule
περι-ποιέω	preserve, protect
περι-ποιέομαι	keep for oneself, acquire
προσ-ποιέομαι	attach to oneself, lay claim to
-ἔμπειρος εἶναι	-profess experience
*ποικίλος	many-colored; various
*ποιμήν, ένος	shepherd
*ποινή	ransom, redemption, recompense[47]
*πόλεμος	war
πολεμικός	(pertaining to war) warlike, hostile[48]
πολέμιος	of or belonging to war, hostile; enemy
πολεμέω	be at war, fight
-τοῖς Ἕλλησι	-with the Greeks

---

43. plutocracy   44. r. πνεϝ-   45. pneumonia   46. poeta
(loanword from Greek; the old word is vates)   47. poena
(perhaps borrowed from the Greek); pain   48. polemical

*πολιός	white, grey[49]
*ἡ πόλις, εως	city, state[50]
πολίτης	citizen
πολῑτεύω	be a citizen
πολῑτεύομαι	live in a state
πολῑτείᾱ	polity; citizenship[51]
πολῑτικός	befitting a citizen, political; statesman
πολιορκέω	blockade, besiege
πολιορκίᾱ	siege
ἐκ-πολιορκέω	take by siege[52]
*πολύς, πολλή, πολύ	much,,many[53]
πολύ *and* πολλῷ μείζων	much greater
οἱ πολλοί	the many
τὰ πολλά	mostly
πολλάκις	often
πολλαπλάσιος	many times more
πολλαχ-οῦ, -ῇ	many times, in many places
(πολλαχόσε, πολλαχόθεν)	
*πορθέω	destroy, ravage
*ποταμός	river[54]
*πότε	when?; (*encl.*) at anytime
τίς ποτε;	whoever?
ποῦ	where?
πόθεν	whence?
ποῖ	whither?
πῇ, πῶς	how?
πηνίκα	when?
πόσος	how great?; (*pl.*) how many?
ποῖος	of what sort?
πότερος	which of the two?[55]

---

49. pallidus, pale   50. *in the names of many cities*: Tripoli, Constantino-ple, Na-ples; metropolis; Istanbul < εἰς τὴν πόλιν   51. politics, police   52. *2nd part from* τὸ ἕρκος wall, bulwark   53. *perhaps from* plē- (πίμπλημι); polygamy, polyp, Polycrates   54. *perhaps like* "torrent" *from* πέτομαι   55. uter

*πρᾷος *and* πραῦς	mild, gentle
(πραΰνω, ἡ πρᾱότης)	
*πράττω	do, work[56]
-σε χρήματα	-exact payment from you
εὖ-	behave well, do well
ἡ πρᾶξις	doing, activity, transaction[57]
τὸ πρᾶγμα	deed, act
τὰ πράγματα	business, negotiations
πράγματα παρέχω	cause trouble
πραγματεύομαι	be busy, take trouble
δια-πράττομαι	accomplish
συμ-πράττω	do with, help
πολυ-πράγμων	officious, meddling, turbulent
(πολυπραγμοσύνη, πολυπραγμονέω)	
*πρέπω	be clearly seen; be like, suit
πρέπει	it is fitting
ἐκ-πρεπής	distinguished out of all, pre-eminent; unseemly
εὐ-πρεπής	well-looking, goodly; fitting, becoming
μεγαλο-πρεπής	magnificent, splendid
*πρέσβυς *and* πρεσβύτης	old man, elder[58]
πρεσβεύω	be the eldest; be an ambassador
πρεσβεύομαι	send, go as ambassador
πρεσβείᾱ	seniority, embassy
πρεσβευτής (*pl.*) πρέσβεις	ambassador
*πρό	1. before, in front of[59]
(πρὸ τῶν πυλῶν, πρὸ τῆς μάχης)	
	2. for: instead of
(πρὸ τῆς πατρίδος, πρὸ τοῦ πατρός)	
πρότερος	prior (*in place or time*)

---

56. practical (πρακτικός active)   57. praxis
58. presbyter, priest, *F* prêtre   59. prō

(*adv.*) πρότερον	before, earlier, sooner
προτεραίᾱ (ἡμέρᾱ)	the day before
πρίν	until, before
πρῶτος	first, foremost
(πρωτεύω)	
πρωτεῖον	first prize; chief rank
πρωί *and* πρῴ	early, early in the day
πρῴην	lately, recently
πρῴρᾱ	prow
πόρρω *and* πρόσω	(*adv.*) far, farther[60] (*prp.*) far (from)
(πόρρωθεν)	
*πρός	I. (*adv.*) to, toward
πρόσθεν, ἔμπροσθεν	before, in front of
	II. (*prp.*): 1. (*with gen.*) from
πρὸς μεσημβρίας	-the south
πρὸς τῶν ᾿Αθηναίων	on the side of the Athenians
	2. (*with dat.*) at, near
πρὸς τῷ ὄρει	at the foot of the mountain
	3. (*with acc.*) toward, against
κλαίειν πρὸς οὐρανόν	cry to heaven
*πρύμνᾰ *and* πρύμνη	stern
*πρύτανις	prince, ruler, lord
(πρυτανεύω)	
πρυτανεῖον	town hall
*πταίω	make to stumble, err
*πτωχός	beggar
*πυγμή	boxing match[61]
πύκτης	boxer
*πυκνός	close, thick; frequent
*πύλη	gate, door[62]
πυλωρός	gatekeeper[63]
*πυνθάνομαι	ask, inquire, understand

---

60. porrō 61. pugnus, pugna, pygmy, *F* poing 62. Πύλαι: *name of several passes, for example* Thermopylae; propylaea
63. ὁράω

-αὐτῶν τὸ αἴτιον	-ask them the cause
-αὐτοὺς τετρωμένους	-learn that they were wounded
*τὸ πῦρ	fire[64]
ἡ πυρά	pyre
πυρετός	fever
*πύργος	tower
*πῡρός	wheat
*πωλέω	sell
-πολλοῦ	-at a high price
*πῶλος	young animal, foal[65]

P

*ἡ ῥάβδος	rod, stick[1]
*ῥᾴδιος	easy, light[2]
ῥᾴθῡμος	easy tempered; thoughtless
(ῥᾳθῡμέω, ῥᾳθῡμίᾱ)	
*ῥέω	flow, run[3]
ῥεῦμα	flow, stream[4]
ῥοή *and* ῥοῦς	river, stream
ῥυθμός	measured motion *or* time; proportion[5]
*ῥήγνῡμι	break (*tr.*)[6]
*τὸ ῥῆμα	(*that which is said*) word, speech, tale[7]
ῥήτωρ, ορος	orator
(ῥητεύω, ῥητορικός)	
παρρησίᾱ	freedom of speech, frankness[8]
*τὸ ῥῖγος	cold; shivering from cold[9]
ῥῑγόω	be cold
*ῥίζα	root[10]
*ῥῑπτω	throw
*ἡ ῥίς, ῥῑνός	nose (*usu. in pl.*)[11]

---

64. pyrotechnics; *cp.* pūrus (*namely* bright, clear)
65. pullus, pullet   1. verberare   2. *cp.* lĕvis   3. *r.*
ῥευ-, ῥεϝ-, ῥυ-; catarrh, diarrhea   4. rheum, rheumatism
5. rhythm   6. wreck   7. *r.* Ϝερ-, Ϝρη-: ἐρῶ, εἴρηκα;
verbum   8. πᾶν   9. frigus, frigid, *F* froid   10. radix,
radish   11. rhinoceros (κέρας)

*ῥόδον	rose[12]
*ῥώννῡμι	make strong
ἐρρωμένος	strong
ἔρρωσο	be strong[13]
ῥώμη	strength, might
ἄρρωστος	weak, sick
(ἀρρωστέω)	

Σ

*ἡ σάλπιγξ, γγος	trumpet, trumpet call
σαλπίζω	sound the trumpet
(ὁ σαλπιγκτής)	
*ἡ σάρξ, σαρκός	flesh[1]
(σαρκώδης)	
*σατράπης	satrap (Persian governor)
*σαφής	clear, distinct; sure
(ἀ-σαφής)	
σαφηνίζω	make clear, explain
*σβέννῡμι	quench
σβέννυμαι	be quenched
ἀ-σβεστος	unquenchable[2]
*σέβω and σέβομαι	worship, honor
Σεβαστός	Augustus
εὐ-σεβής	pious
(εὐσεβέω)	
εὐ-σέβεια	piety
ἀ-σεβής	impious
(ἀσεβέω, ἀσέβεια)	
σεμνός	august, solemn[3]
ἡ σεμνότης	solemnity, dignity
σεμνῡνομαι	be pompous, haughty
*σείω	shake, move to and fro
σεισμός	shock, earthquake[4]

---

12. *loanword*; rosa   13. *cp.* vale   1. sarcophagus (λίθος
σαρκοφάγος *a lime-stone which quickly consumed animal sub-
stances*); sarcastic (σαρκάζω *bite the lips in rage*)
2. asbestos   3. < σεβ-νός   4. seismograph

σεισάχθεια	shaking off of burdens[5]
*σελήνη	moon
*τὸ σῆμα *and* σημεῖον	sign, token
σημαίνω	give a sign; signify
*σήπω	make rotten
σήπομαι	become rotten[6]
*τὸ σθένος	power, might
ἀ-σθενής	powerless, sick[7]
(ἀσθενέω, ἀσθένεια)	
*σῑγή *and* σιωπή	silence
σῑγάω *and* σιωπάω	be silent
*σίδηρος	(*noun*) iron
σίδηροῦς	(*adj*.) iron
*σῖτος *and* σῖτίον	grain, bread[8]
ἡ σῖτησις	feeding, eating
ἐπι-σῑτίζομαι	provide oneself with food
*σκάπτω	dig a trench[9]
τὸ σκάφος	a digging; (hull of a ship)
*σκεδάννῡμι	scatter
*τὸ σκέλος	leg[10]
*σκέπτομαι	look carefully at, examine[11]
ἡ σκέψις *and* τὸ σκέμμα	consideration, doubt, perception[12]
σκοπέω (*and med.*)	look at, oversee
σκοπός	one who watches, lookout; mark[13]
ἐπί-σκοπος	overseer[14]
*σκευή	equipment, dress
τὸ σκεῦος	vessel; (*pl.*) tools, military baggage
κατα- *and* παρασκευάζω	prepare
παρα-σκευάζομαι	make preparations

---

5. τὸ ἄχθος; remission of debts under Solon's rule in
Athens   6. septic   7. neurasthenic; *Greek names with*
-σθένης: Δημοσθένης   8. παράσιτος tablefellow   9. shovel
10. τὰ μακρὰ σκέλη the long walls (Athens--Piraeus); *skel-
eton belongs to* σκέλλω dry up (*cp.* σκληρός)   11. < σπεκ-,
cp. specio   12. scepticism   13. *compounds with* -scope
14. bishop; *cp.* inspector

*σκηνή	tent, stage[15]
σκηνόω (*and med.*)	encamp
*σκήπτω	prop, support
σκήπτομαι	lean upon, depend on
ἡ σκῆψις	pretext
σκῆπτρον	walking stick, staff[16]
*σκιά	shade, shadow
(σκιόεις, σκιοειδής)	
*σκληρός	hard, dry[17]
*ὁ *and* τὸ σκότος	darkness[18]
(σκοτώδης)	
σκοτεινός	dark
σκοταῖος	dark, in the dark
κατέβη ἤδη σκοταῖος	he came down after dark
*τὸ σκῦτος	hide, leather[19]
*σοφός	wise, clever
σοφίᾱ	wisdom[20]
σοφίζω	make wise, instruct
σοφίζομαι	devise, contrive
σόφισμα	invention, artifice
σοφιστής	master of one's craft; Sophist
(σοφιστεύω, σοφιστικός)	
*σπανίζω	be rare, scarce; be in want of
-τῶν ἐπιτηδείων	-the necessities of life
σπάνιος	rare, few
*σπάω	draw, pull
*σπείρω	sow
τὸ σπέρμα	seed
σπορός, άδος	scattered[21]
(*adv.* σποράδην)	
*σπένδω	pour out a libation[22]
σπένδομαι	make a treaty

---

15. scaena, scene   16. sceptre   17. arteriosclerosis
18. shade, shadow   19. scutum, *F* écu, esquire   20. Hagia
Sophia, *church in Constantinople in honor of divine wisdom*
21. spores   22. spondeo; *but* spende *from Latin* expendere

-σοι	-with you
σπονδή	drink-offering, libation
σπονδαί (pl.)	solemn treaty, truce
*σπεύδω and σπουδάζω	hasten, urge on
σπουδή	haste; eagerness
σπουδαῖος	zealous
*στάδιον	race course; stade[23]
*στέγω	cover (closely), shelter, protect[24]
τὸ στέγος and ἡ στέγη	roof; house[25]
*στείβω	tread (on), walk[26]
*στέλλω	put in order; send
στολή	a fitting out; garment[27]
στόλος	armed expedition; army, fleet[28]
ἀπό-στολος	messenger; expedition[29]
ἐπι-στέλλω	(send to) bid, enjoin, command
ἐπι-στολή	command; letter[30]
στήλη	post, stele
*στενός	narrow, straight[31]
(ἡ στενότης)	
*στένω and στενάζω	groan
στόνος and στεναγμός	groaning, sighing
(στονόεις)	
*στέργω	love, be fond of
*στερέω and ἀπο-στερέω	rob, deprive
-ὑμᾶς τῶν ἡδονῶν (or τὰς ἡδονάς)	-you of your pleasures
στέρομαι	be deprived of
*στέφω and στεφανόω	crown
τὸ στέμμα	wreath
στέφανος	crown[32]
*τὸ στῆθος	breast, chest
*στίζω	prick, puncture, brand[33]

---

23. *about* 185 *meters*   24. tego, deck   25. tectum, *F* toit
26. stiff   27. stola, stole   28. *cp.* agmen   29. apostle
30. epistula, *F* épître   31. stenography   32. Stephen
33. *r.* στιγ-, di-stinguo, in-stīgo

114

τὸ στίγμα	prick, brand[34]
*στοά	colonnade, stoa[35]
*τὸ στόμα	mouth, face[36]
στόμαχος	throat, stomach[37]
*ὁ στρατός, ἡ στρατιά, and τὸ στράτευμα	army
στρατιώτης (στρατιωτικός)	soldier
στρατεύω and -ομαι	serve as a soldier
στρατείᾱ	campaign; military service
στρατηγός (στρατηγέω, στρατηγίᾱ, στρατηγικός)	general[38]
στρατόπεδον	camp; army[39]
στρατοπεδεύω (and med.)	make camp
*στρέφω	turn, twist, bend
στροφή	turning[40]
στρεπτός	twisted[41]
ἀνα-στρέφω	turn around (tr. and itr.)
κατα-στρέφομαι	subject, subdue
κατα-στροφή	overthrowing, subduing[42]
*στρώννῡμι and στόρνῡμι	stretch out, strew[43]
τὸ στρῶμα	(that which is spread out) (pl.) bedding[44]
κατα-στρώννῡμι	spread, cover
*στυγέω	hate[45]
στυγνός and στυγερός	hated
*σῦκον	fig[46]
σῦκο-φάντης (σῦκοφαντέω)	common informer, false accuser[47]
*σῦλάω	rob, take away[48]
-τὴν θεὰν τοὺς στεφάνους	-the crowns from the goddess

---

34. stigma   35. Στοά ποικίλη, the "painted" stoa, school of the Stoics   36. G Stimme   37. F estomac   38. ἄγω
39. see πέδον   40. strophe   41. cp. torquis from torqueo
42. catastrophe (turning point in a drama)   43. sterno
44. cp. via strata, G Strasse   45. styx   46. cp. ficus
47. one who informed against persons exporting figs from Attica   48. a-sylum

*σύν	with
*σῦς *and* ὗς	swine[49]
*συχνός	long; many; frequent
*σφαῖρα	ball; sphere[50]
(σφαιρο-ειδής)	
*σφάλλω	make to fall, foil[51]
σφάλλομαι ἐλπίδος	my hope is dashed
σφαλερός	making to fall, precarious
ἀ-σφαλής	firm, steadfast[52]
ἀ-σφάλεια	firmness, stability
*σφάττω	slay, sacrifice
(σφαγή, σφαγεύς)	
σφάγιον	victim, sacrifice (*usu. pl.*)
*σφενδόνη	sling[53]
σφενδονάω	sling
(ὁ σφενδονήτης)	
*σφοδρός	vehement
(*adv.*) σφόδρα	very, very much
*σχεδίᾱ	skiff, light boat
*σχίζω	split[54]
*τὸ σῶμα	body, life; person
*σῶος *and* σῶς	safe, sound
σῴζω	save, preserve
σωτήρ ῆρος	savior
(ἡ σώτειρα)	
σωτηρίᾱ	a saving, means of safety
τὰ σωτήρια	offering in return for safety
σώ-φρων	of sound mind,[55] prudent
(σω-φρονέω)	
σω-φροσύνη	moderation, self-control

---

49. sus; hyena (ὕαινα *after* λέαινα lioness)   50. hemi-sphere (ἥμισυς)   51. fallo, fail, *F* faillir   52. *not related to* asphalt (ἄσφαλτος bitumen)   53. funda   54. sci-n-do; schism   55. one in whom the φρήν is sound

116

*τάλᾱς, αινα, αν	(enduring grief) suffering, patient, unlucky[1]
τάλαντον	(that which bears) balance, scale[2]
τάλαντον	(that which is borne) talent, pound
τλήμων	suffering, patient, unlucky
ἡ τόλμα *and* τόλμη	(that which endures) boldness, recklessness
τολμάω	dare, hazard
(τὸ τόλμημα)	
τολμηρός	daring, bold
*ταμίᾱς, ου	distributer, steward
(ταμιεύω)	
*ταπεινός	low, humble
ταπεινόω	make low, humiliate
(ἡ ταπεινότης)	
*ταράττω	disturb, trouble (*tr.*)
ταραχή	disorder, trouble
(ταραχώδης)	
ἀ-τάρακτος	calm, steady
ἀ-ταραξίᾱ	calmness[3]
*τάττω	put in order, arrange[4]
ἡ τάξις	an arranging; order; military unit, battle line
ἐπι- *and* προστάττω	set over, appoint; command, order
(τὸ ἐπίταγμα, τὸ πρόσταγμα)	
ἄ-τακτος	undisciplined, lawless
(ἀτακτέω, ἀταξίᾱ; *opp.* εὔτακτος, εὐταξίᾱ)	
*ταῦρος	bull[5]
*τὸ τάχος	speed[6]
ταχύς	swiftly
(ταχῠ́νω)	

---

1. *r.* ταλα-, τλᾱ-, τολ-; τλῆναι bear, suffer; tollo < tolno; A-tlas   2. *as a measure of weight, approx. 26 kilos (Attic), as money, about $15.00 (cp.* μνᾶ)   3. *a stoic principle*   4. tactics, syntax   5. minotaur; taurus, *F* taureau   6. *r.* θαχ-

ἡ ταχυτής	swiftness
τάχα (adv.)	quickly, soon; perhaps
τὴν ταχίστην and ὡς τάχιστα	as swiftly as possible
ἐπειδὴ τάχιστα	as soon as
*τείνω	stretch[7]; (itr.) extend
τόνος	stretching; cord[8]
*τὸ τεῖχος	wall, fortification[9]
τειχίζω	build a wall
τοῖχος	wall (of a house)
*τεκμαίρομαι	fix by a mark, ordain; infer, conclude
τεκμήριον	sign, token, mark
*τέκτων, ονος	woodworker, artisan[10]
τέχνη	art, craft, science[11]
τεχνίτης	artist, craftsman
ἀ-τεχνῶς	artlessly, simply
*τέλλω, usu. ἀνα-τέλλω	rise, arise
ἀνα-τολή	sunrise, east[12]
ἐν-τέλλομαι (ἐντολή)	enjoin, command
*τὸ τέλος	1. end, purpose[13]
(τὸ) τέλος (adv.)	at last, finally
τέλειος, τέλεος and ἐν-τελής	complete, perfect
τελευταῖος	last, at the end
ἕψομαι-	I will follow to the end
τὸ τελευταῖον (adv.)	lastly
τελευτή	end, fulfillment
τελευτάω	bring to an end; die
δια-τελέω	fulfill; continue doing
-πειρώμενος	-go on trying

---

7. teneo, ten-do, tenuis, thin, F tendre, G dünn; hypotenuse (ὑποτείνουσα γραμμή: *the side of a right-angled triangle that is opposite the right angle*)   8. sound (the stretched string)   9. dough, G Teig; fingo, figura; τεῖχος *orig.* a loam-wall   10. texo weave, braid; F tisser   11. < τεκνᾱ   12. Anatolia (*cp.* Orient)   13. *There are 2 stems in* τέλος: 1. qel- in πέλομαι be in motion, turn; 2. τελα- (*from* τλῆναι), *cp.* τάλας

*τὸ τέλος	2. (burden:) duty; office
εὐ-τελής	cheap, worthless
πολυ-τελής	costly, extravagant
οἱ ἐν τέλει	(those in office) authorities
	for both 1 and 2:
τελέω	complete, accomplish
ἀ-τελής	unfinished
*τέμνω	cut[14]
(ἡ τμῆσις)	
τὸ τμῆμα *and* ἡ τομή	cut, cutting
τὸ τέμενος	(circumscribed area) sacred; temple precinct
ἀπό-τομος	cut off, rough-edged
σύν-τομος	cut short
ἄ-τομος	uncut[15]
λιθο-τομίᾱ	(*usu. pl.*) stone-quarry
*τέρπω	delight, please
ἡ τέρψις	enjoyment
τερπνός	enjoyable, delightful
*τὸ τεῦχος	tool; (*pl.*) weapons
*τέως	so long; a long time; (*also* = ἕως) so long as
*τήκω	melt[16]
τήκομαι	pine away
*τηνικάδε, τηνικαῦτα	at this time
*τίθημι	put, place[17]
-νόμον	-make a law
τίθεμαι τὰ ὅπλα	put down one's arms
τὸ θέμα	something set, theme
ἡ θέσις	setting; position[18]
θεσμός	law, rule; institution
ἀνα-τίθημι	set up; (set up a votive offering) dedicate

14. *r.* τεμ-, τμη-; ἔντομον insectum; entomology, anatomy 15. atom 16. tabes; thaw, *G* taue 17. *r.*: θη-, θε-; to do; făcio, fēci; abdo, condo, credo; *to* ἀποθήκη "storehouse": apothecary, *F* boutique, *Italian* bodega 18. thesis, *and various compounds with it*

τὸ ἀνά-θημα	votive
δια-τίθημι	order, arrange; dispose
δια-θήκη	a disposition *of property by will*, will and testament; covenant
ἐπι-τίθεμαι	put a hand to, undertake
-ἔργῳ	-work
-τοῖς ἀπιοῦσι	-seize those who are leaving
μετα-τίθημι	place differently, change
(ἡ μετάθεσις)	
συν-τίθεμαι	put together; observe; arrange
-αὐτῷ μισθόν	-a wage with him
συν-θήκη	contract, covenant, treaty
ὑπο-τίθημι	lay down, pledge, propose
ὑπο-θήκη	advice, teaching; pledge[19]
ἡ ὑπό-θεσις	basis, hypothesis
*τίκτω	bring forth, bear[20]
τέκνον	child
τόκος	birth; (that which is born) child; interest (*financial*)
οἱ τοκεῖς	parents
*τῑμή	(estimate) price, worth, honor; office; punishment
τῑμιος *and* ἔν-τῑμος	valued, honored
ἄ-τῑμος (*opp.* ἐπί-τῑμος)	not valued, dishonored
ἀ-τῑμίᾱ	dishonor, disrespect
ἀ-τῑμάζω	dishonor
τῑμάω	value, honor, prize
ἐπι-τῑμάω	honor; appraise
(ὁ ἐπιτῑμητής)	
προ-τιμάω	prefer, honor above
τῑμωρός	helping, avenging[21]
τῑμωρέω	help, aid, avenge
τῑμωρέομαι	avenge oneself on, punish

---

19. hypothesis   20. < τι-τκ-ω; *r.*: τεκ-, τοκ-, τκ-
21. < τιμα-Ϝορος preserving honor; *cp.* vindico liberate, protect

-τὸν ἀδικοῦντα	-the wrongdoer
τῑμωρίᾱ	help; retribution, punishment
*τίνω	pay a price *or* penalty
(ἡ τίσις)	
τίνομαι	avenge oneself, punish another
*τίς; τί;	who, what, which?[22]
τί γάρ	why, what then?
τις, τι	someone, something, a certain one
εἴποι ἄν τις	one might say
εἶπόν τινες	some said
λέγεις τι	you are saying something noteworthy
ἀθῡμίᾱ τις	a certain faintheartedness
δεινή τις δύναμις	a terrible power
*τιτρώσκω *and* τραυματίζω	wound
τὸ τραῦμα	wound; defeat
*τοι (*encl.*)	certainly, accordingly[23]
τοι-γάρ, τοι-γαρ-οῦν *and* τοι-γάρ-τοι	therefore
τοί-νυν	so then, now; further
*τόξον	bow
τοξεύω	shoot with a bow
(ὁ τοξότης)	
τὸ τόξευμα	arrow
*τόπος	place[24]
ἄ-τοπος	strange, unnatural, absurd
*τρᾱχύς	rough, hard
(ἡ τρᾱχύτης)	
*τρέπω	turn
τρέπομαι (*med.*)	betake oneself, turn oneself to flight; be changed[25]
τρόπος	turn, direction;[26] fashion, mode, character

---

22. *r.* qui-: quis, quid, *F* que, quoi   23. *older dative of* τύ = σύ   24. topography, utopia: "no place"   25. *aor.* ἐτρεψάμην put to flight; *but* ἐτραπόμην, ἐτράπην fled   26. tropics

παντὶ τρόπῳ	in every way
τροπή	turning, flight
τρόπαιον	(turning point) trophy of victory[27]
ἐπι-τρέπω	(turn to) entrust to, rely on; yield
ἐπί-τροπος	trustee
προ-τρέπω	exhort, persuade
*τρέφω	nourish, rear
(ὁ τροφεύς)	
ἡ τροφός	nurse
τροφή	nourishment
*τρέχω	run
τροχός	(runner) wheel
τρόχος	course
*τρέω	tremble, dread[28]
*τρῐ́βω	rub (off), wear out[29]
τριβή	rubbing; practice; delay
δια-τρῐ́βω	spend time, discuss
δια-τριβή	waste of time, discussion
*τριήρης	trireme[30]
τριήρ-αρχος	captain of a trireme
τριηρ-αρχίᾱ	commanding a trireme
*τρυφή	softness, luxury
τρυφάω	live in luxury
*τρώγω	gnaw, chew
*τυγχάνω	happen, obtain
-σκοποῦ	-hit the mark
(opp. ἀποτυγχάνω)	
-συγγνώμης	-obtain a pardon
-παρών	-happen to be there
ὁ τυχών	any chance person
τύχη	fortune, luck, happenstance[31]
ἀγαθῇ τύχῃ	good luck
εὐ-τυχής	successful, lucky

---

27. trophy, F trophée 28. terreo 29. tero, trivi, rub, grind 30. *a galley with 3 banks of oars* 31. *cp.* fortuna; Τύχη goddess of fate

(εὐτυχέω)

εὐ-τυχίᾱ   success, luck

   (ἀ-τυχής, ἀτυχίᾱ, ἀτυχέω)

   (δυσ-τυχής, δυστυχίᾱ,
   δυστυχέω)

ἐν-, ἐπι-, περι-,   befall; meet with, converse
συν-τυγχάνω   with

  -κώμαις   -befall villages

  -τοῖς φύλαξι   -meet with the guards

* τύμβος   tomb

* τύπτω   strike, beat

τύπος   stroke; form, type

* τύραννος   tyrant[32]

   (τυραννεύω, τυραννέω,
   τυρραννικός)

ἡ τυραννίς   tyranny

* τυφλός   blind[33]

   (ἡ τυφλότης, τυφλόω)

                       Υ

* ἡ ὕβρις   insolence, contempt, arro-
              gance

ὑβρίζω   be contemptuous, arrogant;
              outrage

ὑβριστής   unbridled; an insolent person

* ὑγιής   sound, healthy

ὑγίεια   health

ὑγιεινός   wholesome, sound[1]

ὑγιαίνω   be sound, healthy

* ὑγρός   wet, moist[2]

   (ἡ ὑγρότης)

* τὸ ὕδωρ, ὕδατος   water[3]

ὕδρᾱ   water serpent, Hydra

ἄν-υδρος   lacking water

* υἱός *and* ὑός   son

* ὕλη   wood, matter[4]

---

32. tyrannus, tyrant   33. *G* taub, deaf   1. hygiene; ὑγιής,
ὑγιεινός, *cp*. sanus, saluber   2. humidus; hygrometer
3. unda; hydrant; κλεψύδρα (κλέπτω) waterclock   4. silva

*ὕμνος	song of praise[5]
ὑμνέω	sing; hymn
ὑμέναιος	wedding song
*ὑπέρ	1. (*with gen.*) over, for[6]
(ὑπὲρ τῆς γῆς· ὑπὲρ τῆς πατρίδος μάχεσθαι)	
	2. (*with acc.*) over, beyond
(ὑπὲρ τὸν Ἑλλήσποντον οἰκεῖν)	
ὑπὲρ ἄνθρωπον	beyond the nature of man
ὕπερθεν	from above, thereupon
ὕπατος	highest; consul[7]
*ὕπνος	sleep[8]
ἐν-ύπνιον	dream[9]
ἀγρ-υπνίᾱ	insomnia
*ὑπό	1. (*with gen.*) under, (*with*) *pass.*) by[10]
ὑπὸ στέγης	under the roof
ὑπὸ τοῦ πολεμίου πιέζομαι	be crushed by the enemy
ὑπὸ λύπης	in pain
	2. (*with dat.*) under, below
ὑπὸ γῇ εἶναι	be under the earth
ὑπὸ τοῖς Πέρσαις γίγνεσθαι	be under the sway of the Persians
	3. (*with acc.*) towards and under; about
ὑπὸ γῆν ἐλθεῖν	go under the earth
ὑπὸ νύκτα	toward evening
*ὕστερος	later, following
(*adv.* ὕστερον)	
ὑστεραίᾱ	the following day
ὑστερέω	come later, too late, remain behind
-τῆς μάχης	-come too late for the battle
-σοῦ	-stand behind you
*ὑφαίνω	weave, spin
(ὁ ὑφάντης)	

5. hymn   6. super, *F* sur   7. summus < sup-mos   8. < ὕπνος; somnus < sopnos; hypnosis   9. somnium   10. sub

τὸ ὕφασμα	web
*τὸ ὕψος	top
(ὑψό-θεν)	
ὑψηλός	high, lofty
*ὔω	rain
(Ζεύς) ὕει	it is raining

Φ

*φαιδρός	bright, radiant
*φαίνω	make to appear, bring to light[1]
φαίνομαι	show oneself, seem, appear
-νοσῶν	-it is clear that I am sick[2]
-νοσεῖν	-it appears that I may be sick
ἀπο-φαίνω	show forth, declare, prove
ἀπο-φαίνομαι	make a display of, explain
-ἔργα	-finish the work
ἐμ-φανής, κατα-φανής	manifest, clear
ἐπι-φανής	clear, coming to light[3]
φανερός	obvious
-εἰμι ποιῶν	-I am acting openly
ἀ-φανής	unclear
ἀ-φανίζω	hide, suppress, obscure, efface
*ἡ φάλαγξ, γγος	phalanx[4]
*φάρμακον	medicine, magic, poison[5]
*φαῦλος, φλαῦρος	light, trivial; poor, common[6]
*φείδομαι	spare, be sparing of
-ἵππων, σίτου	-horses, grain
*φέρω	carry, bear[7]
φέρομαι	(pass.) hurry; (med.) get for oneself
φέρε εἰπέ	come, speak

---

1. phenomenon, fantasy (φαντασία), fancy   2. cp. δοκῶ
νοσῶν = a) I appear to be sick (= be sick), b) I give the
appearance of being sick   3. festival of Epiphany
4. i.e. heavy-armed infantry in close and deep ranks
5. pharmacy, F pharmacie   6.   φλαῦλος (dissimilation as
in singularis < singulalis)   7. fero, fertilis

φέρω χαλεπῶς	do poorly, be unlucky
-ἀπεστερημένος	-having been robbed
-τοῖς πράγμασι	-in one's affairs
φέρων πολλὴν λείαν	carrying off much booty
φόρος *and* φορά	(that which is carried) tribute
φορτίον	burden, load
φορτικός	burdensome
φαρέτρᾱ	quiver
φώρ	thief
ἀνα-φέρω	bring, report, carry up (back)
δια-φέρω	differ; carry over, across[8]
-ἄλλων	-differ from others
οὐδὲν διαφέρει	it makes no difference
δια-φερόντως	differently; especially
δια-φέρομαι	be at variance with, quarrel with
-ἄλλοις	-others
διά-φορος	different
διαφορά	(difference) distinction
συμ-φέρει	it is useful, expedient
συμ-φορά	chance; misfortune[9]
ὁ ἀμ(φι)φορεύς	two-handled jar, amphora
δίφρος	(carrying two:) wagon, chariot
*φεύγω	flee[10]
-τὸν ὄλεθρον	-the destruction
-ἀσεβείας	-be charged with impiety; be banished
φυγή	flight, banishment[11]
φυγάς, άδος	fugitive
φυγαδεύω	banish
ἀπο-φεύγω	flee from, escape; be acquitted
κατα-φεύγω (καταφυγή)	take flight, refuge

---

8. differre, *F* différer   9. *cp.* fortuna *and* τύχη
10. fugio; *F* fuir   11. fuga

*φημί, φάσκω	say, allege, think[12]
οὔ φημι	say no, deny
ἡ πρό-φασις	ground, pretext
πρόφασιν *and* προφάσει	as one pretends, for a show
φήμη	voice, word[13]
εὔ-φημος	auspicious, of good omen
(εὐφημέω)	
φωνή	sound, voice[14]
(ἄφονος)	
*φθάνω	anticipate; come before
-τοὺς πολεμίους ἀφικόμενος	-arrive before the enemy
*φθέγγομαι	utter a sound; advise, call
φθόγγος *and* τὸ φθέγμα	voice, language[15]
τὸ ἀπό-φθεγμα	utterance, sententious answer
*φθείρω, (*usu.*) διαφθείρω	spoil, ruin, destroy
*φθίνω	decline, waste away
*φθόνος	envy, ill-will
φθονέω	envy, begrudge[16]
-αὐτῷ τῶν χρημάτων	-him his money
φθονοῦμαι	be envied
φθονερός	envious
ἄ-φθονος	without envy
ἀ-φθονίᾱ	freedom from envy
ἐπί-φθονος	liable to envy[17]
*φίλος	friend, lover
φιλέω	love
-σιγᾶν	-be fond of being silent
φίλιος	friendly
φιλίᾱ	love, friendship
φιλ-άργυρος	lover of money
φιλό-νῑκος (φιλονῑκίᾱ, φιλονῑκέω)	(fond of victory) striving for victory

---

12. fāri, fātum, fateor   13. fāma, fame   14. *used in
compounds* - phone   15. mono-phthong, di-phthong   16. *but:*
invideo divitiis eius   17. *cp.* invidiōsus (*but* invidus,
invīsus)

φιλό-σοφος (φιλοσοφίᾱ, φιλοσοφέω)	lover of wisdom, philosopher
φιλό-τῑμος	ambitious, lover of honor
φιλο-τῑμία	ambition, love of honor
φιλο-τῑμέομαι	love honor; be ambitious
*φλυᾱρέω	play the fool
φλυᾱρίᾱ	folly
*φόβος (ἄφοβος)	fear
φοβερός	fearful
φοβέω	frighten[18]
φοβέομαι	be afraid
-μὴ κακῶς πάσχωμεν	-lest we fare ill
-εἰπεῖν	-to speak
*ὁ φοῖνιξ, ῑκος	purple; palm; the phoenix
φοινῑκοῦς	purple, crimson
*φοιτάω	go to and fro, range about
*φόνος (φονεύς)	murder[19]
φονεύω	be a murderer; murder
*φράζω	point out, say
φράζομαι	muse over, ponder
ἡ φράσις	expression[20]
*ἡ φρήν	(diaphragm) sense, under-standing; heart[21]
φρένες	seat of life[22]
μετά-φρενον	broad of the back[23]
φρενόω	make wise, instruct
φρόνιμος	discreet, understanding
φρονέω	be wise, think
-τὰ Φιλίππου	-keep Philip's affairs in mind
κατα-φρονέω	despise, disdain[24]
-τῶν θεῶν	-the gods

---

18. cp. vereor with nē or the inf.   19. fendo in offendo, defendo   20. phrase   21. r. φρεν-, φρον-, φρη-; schizophrenic (σχίζω)   22. considered to be the location of the soul   23. behind the diaphragm or midriff   24. cp. despicio

μέγα φρονέω	be high-minded
ἡ φρόνησις	high-mindedness; thought-fulness, prudence
τὸ φρόνημα	mind, will, spirit
εὔ-φρων, ονος	cheerful
(εὐφροσύνη)	
εὐ-φραίνω	cheer
ἄ-φρων	foolish
(ἀφροσύνη)	
ἡ φροντίς, ίδος	thought, care
φροντίζω	think, consider
-αὐτῶν	-them
*φύλαξ, κος	guard
φυλακή	watch
φυλάττω	guard, keep safe
φυλάττομαι	be on one's guard
-κόλακας	-for flatterers[25]
*φύλλον	leaf[26]
*φύω	make grow, bring forth, produce[27]
φύομαι	grow
πέφῡκα	be so by nature, be
ἡ φύσις	(growth) nature[28]
φυτόν	plant
φυτεύω	plant
φῦλον	stem, race
φῡλή	tribe[29]
εὐ-φυής	well-grown, shapely
ὑπερ-φυής	over-sized
*τὸ φῶς, φωτός	light[30]

---

25. *cp.* caveo adulatores   26. < φύλϳον, folium, *F* feuille
27. fio, fui, to be   28. physiology, physics (φυσικὴ
τέχνη)   29. *in Attica, first 4 tribes, then 10 after
Cleisthenes; cp.* tribus   30. < φάϝος, *perhaps from*
φαίνω; phosphorus (φως-φόρος)

X

*χαίνω	yawn, gape[1]
τὸ χάος	chasm, gulf[2]
*χαίρω	rejoice[3]
-(ἐπὶ) τοῖς ἐπαίνους	-over the praise
-ἀκούσας	-at hearing
χαῖρε	greetings!
χαίρειν ἐάω	put away, renounce
χαρά	joy
ἡ χάρις, ιτος	favor, grace[4]
χάριν ἔχω *and* οἶδα	I have favor[5]
τῶν πολιτῶν χάριν	for the sake of the citizens[6]
Χάριτες	Graces[7]
ἀ-χαρις	ungracious, ungrateful
χαρίεις	graceful
χαριεντίζομαι	speak gracefully, with elegance
χαρίζομαι	show favor
ἀ-χάριστος	ungracious, ungrateful
(ἀχαριστέω)	
ἀ-χαριστία	ingratitude
*χαλεπός	difficult, severe
(ἡ χαλεπότης)	
χαλεπαίνω	be severe, hard
*χαλκός	(*noun*) brass, copper
χαλκοῦς	(*adj.*) copper
χαλκεύς	brazier, coppersmith
(χαλκεύω, χαλκεῖον)	
*χαράττω	sharpen, engrave
ὁ χάραξ, κος	pointed stake
ὁ χαρακτήρ, ῆρος	stamp, mark, character
*τὸ χεῖλος	lip, edge, brim
*ὁ χειμών, ῶνος	winter[8]

---

1. hio   2. chaos   3. < χάρjω; hortor, urge, desire
4. *cp*. gratia   5. *cp*. gratiăm habeo   6. *cp*. civium
gratiā   7. *cp*. Gratiae   8. hiems; (*old Indic*) Himalaya =
snow country

χειμερινός *and* χειμέριος	stormy, wintry
χειμάζω	expose to *or* live through the winter
ἡ χιών, όνος	snow
*ἡ χείρ, χειρός	hand[9]
εἰς χεῖρας ἐλθεῖν	fall into someone's hands
δυσ-χερής	difficult, hard to handle
(ἡ δυσχέρεια)	
εὐ-χερής	quick, ready of hand
(ἡ εὐχέρεια)	
ἐπι- *and* ἐγ-χειρέω	put one's hand to, set to work on
-τοῖς πολεμίοις	-lay hands on the enemy
ἐγ-χειρίζω	put in hand, entrust
ἐγ-χειρίδιον	dagger
χειρόομαι	be taken prisoner
χειρο-τονέω	stretch out the hand[10]
*χέω	pour, shed[11]
χόω	heap up
ἡ χῶσις, τὸ χῶμα	mound, bank
χύτρᾱ *and* χύτρος	earthen pot
συγ-χέω	pour together, mix; confound
*χείρων, ονος	worse
*ὁ χήν, χηνός	goose[12]
*χθές	yesterday[13]
*ἡ χθών, χθονός	earth, ground[14]
χθόνιος	in, under the earth
χαμαί	on the ground[15]
*χίμαιρα	she-goat, chimaera
*ὁ χιτών, ῶνος	undergarment[16]
*ἡ χλαῖνα *and* ἡ χλαμύς, ύδος	outer garment[17]
*χλωρός	pale; green[18]
*χολή *and* χόλος	gall; anger[19]

---

9. *cp.* manus   10. τονέω *from* τείνω   11. *r.* χεϜ-, χοϜ-, χυ-; fundo   12. ᾱnser < hᾱnser; *G* Gans   13. heri
14. humus   15. humi   16. *cp.* tunica (*both* < *Semitic* ki kithuna)   17. *corresponds to the toga*   18. chlorine
19. melan-coly, cholera, *F* colère

χολόω	make angry, embitter
χολόομαι	be angered
*χορός	dance; chorus
χορεύω *and* χορεύομαι	dance, form a chorus
ὁ χορευτής	choral dancer
χορ-ηγός	chorus leader[20]
*χόρτος	feeding-place[21]
*χρίω	anoint[22]
τὸ χρῖμα *and* χρῖσμα	salve, ungent
*χρόνος	time[23]
χρόνιος	after a long time, late, long
*χρῡσός	gold
(χρῡσοειδής)	
χρῡσοῦς	golden
χρῡσίον	gold, money
*I. χρῶ	give an oracle[24]
ἐχρήσθη	it was proclaimed by an oracle
χρῶμαι	consult an oracle
χρησμός *and* χρησμ-ῳδίᾱ	oracular speech[25]
χρησμ-ῳδός	prophet; reciting oracles in verse
(χρησμῳδέω)	
χρηστήριον	seat of an oracle
II. χρῶμαι	use, need
-λόγῳ ἡγεμόνι	-use reason as a guide[26]
χρηστός	useful, needful
τὸ χρῆμα	thing, matter, affair, (*pl.*) goods, money
χρηματίζομαι	transact business
παραχρῆμα (*adv.*)	on the spot, forthwith
ἡ χρῆσις	power *or* means of using, employment
χρήσιμος	useful, serviceable

---

20. ἡγέομαι   21. hortus, garden and yard, *F* jardin, *G* Garten   22. Χριστός, Christophoros *thus* Christopher 23. chronometer, chronic (τὰ χρονικά)   24. < χρῆω furnish the use of something, *i.e.* lend; *cp. also* χείρων < χέριων = deterior   25. ῳδή   26. *cp.* utor (*instrumental*)

χρή	it is necessary[27]
(ἐ)χρῆν σε τῆς μάχης παύσασθαι	it was necessary for you to cease from battle
χρεών	that which is necessary[28]
χρείᾱ	advantage, service
χρῄζω	need, want, lack
*ὁ χρώς, χρωτός	skin, flesh, surface of a body[29]
*χωλός	lame
(χωλεύω)	
*χώρᾱ	place, spot[30]
χῶρος	place, land, country
χωρίον	particular place
χωρέω	make room, give way
ἐπι-χώριος, ἐγ-χώριος	in, of the country, native
ἀνα-χωρέω	retreat, withdraw
προ-χωρέω	advance, go on
συγ-χωρέω	come together, unite[31]
*χωρίς	apart from
-τῶν ἄλλων	-the others
χωρίζω	separate, part
-τῶν τεχνῶν	-from the arts

Ψ

*ψαύω	touch
*ψέγω	blame
ψόγος	blame
*ψεύδω	cheat, beguile
ψεύδομαι	(med.) lie, deceive, falsify; (pass.) be cheated
-ἐλπίδος	-in a hope
τὸ ψεῦδος	lie
ψευδής	untrue, lying, false
ψεύστης	liar, cheat
*ἡ ψῆφος	pebble

---

27. *actually an old noun*: need, necessity, demand
28. *ptc.*: χρή *and* ὄν   29. *thus* chrome   30. country, *as opposed to* city   31. *cp.* cedo: concedo

ψηφίζομαι	vote (with a pebble)
τὸ ψήφισμα	proposition
ἀπο-ψηφίζομαι	reject
κατα-ψηφίζομαι	vote against, condemn
-αὐτοῦ θάνατον	-him to death
*ψῑλός	bare, naked
ψῑλοί	light troops
ψῑλόω	strip bare
*ψύχω	breathe, blow
τὸ ψῦχος	cold, chill
ψῡχρός	cold, frigid
ψῡχή	soul; life[1]

Ω

*ὠθέω	thrust, push, shove
*ὠμός	raw, unripe[1]
(ἡ ὠμότης)	
*ὦμος	shoulder[2]
*ὠνέομαι	buy; bribe[3]
ὠνή	buying, purchase
ὤνιος	for sale
τὰ ὤνια	goods for sale
*ὥρᾱ	hour, proper time[4]
ὡραῖος	ripe, mature, seasonable
ὀπ-ώρᾱ	late summer[5]
*ὡς	1. (adv.) so, thus, as (see ὅς) 2. (cj.) that, so that, in order that
*ὠτειλή	wound, scar

---

1. psych-iatrist (ἰατρός), psychologist; cp. also spiro, spiritus 1. amārus 2. umerus 3. r. Ϝων-; vēn-do, vēn-eo; F vendre 4. hora; horoscope 5. ὀπ(ισθεν) and ὥρα

ALPHABETICAL INDEX TO PART C

This index is designed to aid in the search for words in Part C whose derivation is not readily ascertainable

A

ἄβατος : βαίνω
ἀγνοέω : γιγνώσκω
ἀγνώμων : γιγνώσκω
ἀγορά : ἀγείρω
ἀγορεύω : ἀγείρω
ἄγροικος : ἄγω
ἀγρός : ἄγω
ἀγρυπνία : ὕπνος
ἀγών : ἄγω
ἀδεής : δέδοικα
ἄδικος : δείκνυμι
ἄδυτον : δύω
αἰεί : ἀεί
αἰκία : εἴκω II
αἰών : ἀεί
ἄκλαυτος : κλαίω
ἀκολασία : κολάζω
ἀκόντιον : ἀκμή
ἄκρα : ἀκμή
ἄκρατος : κεράννυμι
ἀκροάομαι : ἀκμή
ἀκτή : ἀκμή
ἀληθής : λανθάνω
ἀλλάττω : ἄλλος
ἀμαθής : μανθάνω
ἀμέλεια : μέλει
ἀμνηστέω : μένος
ἀμφιγνοέω : γιγνώσκω
ἀμφορεύς : φέρω
ἄν : εἰ
ἀναιδής : αἰδέομαι
ἀνάστασις : ἵστημι
ἀνατολή : τέλλω
ἀνδράποδον : ἀνήρ
ἀνδρεῖος : ἀνήρ
ἀνήκεστος : ἀκέομαι
ἀντάω : ἀντί
ἀντίπαλος : πάλη
ἀνώμαλος : ὁμός
ἀνώνυμος : ὄνομα
ἀπαντάω : ἀντί
ἄπειρος (*twice*) : πέρας
ἄπληστος : πίμπλημι

ἀπορέω : πέρας
ἀπόστολος : στέλλω
ἀπότομος : τέμνω
ἀπόφθεγμα : φθέγγομαι
ἀραρίσκω : ἄρα
ἄργος : ἔργον
ἄρθρον : ἄρα
ἄριστος : ἀρετή
ἄρρωστος : ῥώννυμι
ἄσβεστος : σβέννυμι
ἀσθενής : σθένος
ᾆσμα : ἀείδω
ἄσμενος : ἥδομαι
ἀστραπή : ἀστήρ
ἀσφαλής : σφάλλω
αὐδή : ἀείδω
αὐθάδης : ἥδομαι
αὔριον : ἕως
αὐτάρκης : ἀρκέω
αὐτόνομος : νέμω
ἄφρων : φρήν
ἄχαρις : χαίρω

B

βαδίζω : βαίνω
βάσιμος : βαίνω
βέβαιος : βαίνω
βέλος : βάλλω
βιβάζω : βαίνω
βιβρώσκω : βορά
βοηθέω : βοάω
βολή : βάλλω
βουλεύω : βούλομαι
βρῶσις : βορά
βωμός : βαίνω

Γ

γαμβρός : γάμος
γενεά : γίγνομαι

135

γεννάω : γίγνομαι
γένος : γίγνομαι
γεωργός : γῆ
γῆρας : γέρας
γνήσιος : γίγνομαι
γνώμη : γιγνώσκω
γνώριμος : γιγνώσκω
γονεύς : γίγνομαι
γράμμα : γράφω
γωνία : γόνυ

Δ

δειλός : δέδοικα
δειμαίνω : δέδοικα
δεινός : δέδοικα
δέος : δέδοικα
δεσμός : δέω I
δεσπότης : δέμω
δεύτερον : δέω II
διάδημα : δέω I
διαθήκη : τίθημι
διάλεκτος : λέγω
διάλογος : λέγω
διάνοια : νοῦς
διάφορος : φέρω
δίκη : δείκνυμι
δίφρος : φέρω
διῶρυξ : ὀρύττω
δόμος : δέμω
δόξα : δοκέω
δορά : δέρω
δόρυ : δρῦς
δυσχερής : χείρ
δῶρον : δίδωμι

Ε

ἐάν : εἰ
ἔγκλημα : καλέω
ἐγκωμιάζω : κῶμος
ἐδωδή : ἐσθίω
εἶδος : οἶδα
εἴδωλον : οἶδα
εἴθε : εἰ
εἰκών : εἴκω II
εἴμαρται : μέρος
εἰς : ἐν
εἴτε : εἰ
εἴωθα : ἔθος
ἕκαστος : ἑκάς
ἑκάτερος : ἑκάς
ἐκκλησία : καλέω

ἐκποδών : πέδον
ἐκπολιορκέω : πόλις
ἑκών : ἑκούσιος
ἔλασις : ἐλαύνω
ἐμμελής : μέλος
ἔμπειρος : πέρας
ἐμποδίζω : πέδον
ἔμπορος : πέρας
ἐναντίος : ἀντί
ἐναργής : ἄργυρος
ἔνδον : ἐν
ἐνέδρα : ἕδος
ἔνθα : ἐν
ἐνθουσιάζω : θεός
ἐνταῦθα : ἐν
ἐξῆς : ἔχω
ἕξις : ἔχω
ἐπιλήσμων : λανθάνω
ἐπίπονος : πένομαι
ἐπίσκοπος : σκέπτομαι
ἐπιστάτης : ἵστημι
ἐπιστήμη : ἵστημι
ἐπίτροπος : τρέπω
ἐποχή : ἔχω
ἐπώνυμος : ὄνομα
ἐρρωμένος : ῥώννυμι
ἐσθής : ἕννυμι
Εὔβοια : βοῦς
εὐδία : δῖος
εὐήθης : ἔθος
εὐλαβής : λαμβάνω
εὔνοια : νοῦς
εὐφραίνω : φρήν
εὔφρων : φρήν
εὐχερής : χείρ
εὐώνυμος : ὄνομα
εὐωχέω : ἔχω
ἔφηβος : ἥβη

Ζ

ζυγόν : ζεύγνυμι
ζωστήρ : ζώννυμι

Η

ᾗ : ὅς
ἤδη : δή
ἡδύς : ἥδομαι
ἦθος : ἔθος
ἥκιστα : ἥττων
ἤν : εἰ

Θ

θάνατος : θνῄσκω
θάτερον : τὸ ἔτερον
θέλω : ἐθέλω
θέμα : τίθημι
θερμός : θέρος
θεσμός : τίθημι
θεωρός : θέα
θρασύς : θάρσος
θυρωρός : θύρα

Ι

ἰδέα : οἶδα
ἰδρύω : ἕδος
ἱκανός : ἱκνέομαι
ἱκέτης : ἱκνέομαι
ἱμάτιον : ἕννυμι
ἱστορέω : οἶδα
ἰσχύς : ἔχω
ἴσχω : ἔχω

Κ

καθά(περ) : κατά
καθεύδω : εὕδω
κάθημαι : ἧμαι
καθίζω : ἕδος
καίτοι : καί
κακοῦργος : κακός
καλλωπίζω : καλός
καρτερός : κράτος
κατάλογος : λέγω
καταστροφή : στρέφω
κατήγορος : ἀγείρω
κάτοπτρον : ὄψις
καῦμα : καίω
κέκτημαι : κτάομαι
κλαγγή : κλάζω
κλῆσις : καλέω
κλῖμαξ : κλίνω
κλοπή : κλέπτω
κοιμάω : κεῖμαι
κορυφή : κόρυς
κρᾶσις : κεράννυμι
κρατήρ : κεράννυμι
--κρατία : κράτος
κρύβδην : κρύπτω
κτῆμα : κτάομαι
κτῆσις : κτάομαι
κυνηγέτης : κύων

Λ

λάθρα : λανθάνω
λαμπάς : λάμπω
Λάχεσις : λαγχάνω
λῄζω : λεία
λήθη : λανθάνω
ληστής : λεία
λιθοτομία : τέμνω
λογίζομαι : λέγω
λόγος : λέγω
λοιμός : λιμός
λοιπός : λείπω
λουτρόν : λούω
λυσιτελής : λύω

Μ

μά : μήν
μάθημα : μανθάνω
μαθητής : μανθάνω
μαίνομαι : μένος
μανία : μένος
μάντις : μένος
μεῖξις : μείγνυμι
μελέτη : μέλει
μέν : μήν
μεσημβρία : ἡμέρα
μετάνοια : νοῦς
μετάστασις : ἵστημι
μετάφρενον : φρήν
μετέωρος : αἴρω
μέτωπον : ὄψις
μή : οὐ
μῆκος : μακρός
μιαρός : μιαίνω
μίασμα : μιαίνω
μιμνήσκω : μένος
μίσγω : μείγνυμι
μνῆμα : μένος
μοῖρα : μέρος
μομφή : μέμφομαι
μόνιμος : μένω
μόρος : μέρος
μυστήρια : μύω

Ν

ναυαγός : ναῦς
νεανίας : νέος
Νέμεσις : νέμω
νεότης : νέος

νεωστί : νέος
νεωτερίζω : νέος
νοέω : νοῦς
νομή : νέμω
νομίζω : νέμω
νόμος : νέμω
νουθετέω : νοῦς

Ο

ὅδε : ὁ
ὀδμή : ὄζω
ὀδών : ἐσθίω
οἰκτίρω : οἶκτος
οἰμώζω : οἴμοι
οἷος : ὅς
ὄλεθρος : ὄλλυμι
ὀλιγωρέω : ὀλίγος
ὀλκάς : ἕλκω
ὁμαλής : ὁμός
ὄμμα : ὄψις
ὅμοιος : ὁμός
ὁμολογέω : λέγω
ὁμόνοια : νοῦς
ὄνειρος : ὄναρ
ὀπώρα : ὥρα
ὄργανον : ἔργον
ὀργυιά : ὀρέγω
ὀρχήστρα : ὀρχέομαι
ὀσμή : ὄζω
ὅσος : ὅς
ὄστρακον : ὀστέον
ὀσφραίνομαι : ὄζω
ὅτι : ὅς
οὐδέ : οὐ
οὐδείς : οὐ
οὐδέτερος : ἕτερος
οὔκουν : οὖν
οὕνεκα : ἑκούσιος
οὔπω : οὐ
οὐσία : εἰμί
οὔτε : οὐ
οὗτος : ὁ
ὀφθαλμός : ὄψις
ὀφλισκάνω : ὀφείλω
ὀχυρός : ἔχω
ὀψέ : ὄπισθεν

Π

πάγος : πήγνυμι
πάθημα : πάσχω

πάθος : πάσχω
παίζω : παῖς
παλαίστρα : πάλη
πανδημεί : δῆμος
πανήγυρις : ἀγείρω
πανοῦργος : ἔργον
πανταχῇ : πᾶς
παντοῖος : πᾶς
πάνυ : πᾶς
παράδειγμα : δείκνυμι
παράδοξος : δοκέω
παράνοια : νοῦς
παράνομος : νέμω
παραπλήσιος : πέλας
παραχρῆμα : χρῶ
παρουσία : εἰμί
παρρησία : ῥῆμα
πεζός : πέδον
πειθώ : πείθω
πεῖρα : πέρας
πειράομαι : πέρας
πένης : πένομαι
πένθος : πάσχω
πέπρωται : πέρας
περαιόω : πέρας
περιττός : πέριξ
πηδάω : πέδον
πηλίκος : ἧλιξ
πηνίκα : πότε
πιθανός : πείθω
πίστις : πείθω
πλάσμα : πλάττω
πλεονέκτης : ἔχω
πλέως : πίμπλημι
πληγή : πλήττω
πλήθω : πίμπλημι
πλημμελής : μέλος
πλήρης : πίμπλημι
πλησίος : πέλας
πλοῖον : πλέω
πλοῦς : πλέω
πνεῦμα : πνέω
πολυπράγμων : πράττω
πομπή : πέμπω
πονηρός : πένομαι
πόνος : πένομαι
πορεύω : πέρας
πορθμός : πέρας
πορίζω : πέρας
πόρος : πέρας
πόρρω : πρό
πόσος, ποῦ : πότε
ποτόν : πίνω
πούς : πέδον

πρᾶσις : πιπράσκω
πρίν : πρό
πρόβατον : βαίνω
πρόβλημα : βάλλω
προδότης : δίδωμι
προσδοκάω : δέχομαι
προστάτης : ἵστημι
πρόσωπον : ὄψις
πρόφασις : φαίνω
πρῷρα : πρό
πρῶτος : πρό
πτέρον : πέτομαι
πτῶμα : πίπτω
πῶμα : πίνω

P

ῥεῦμα : ῥέω
ῥήτωρ : ῥῆμα
ῥοή : ῥέω
ῥυθμός : ῥέω
ῥώμη : ῥώννυμι

Σ

Σεβαστός : σέβω
σεισμός : σείω
σεμνός : σέβω
σιωπάω : σιγή
σκάφος : σκάπτω
σκέψις : σκέπτομαι
σκῆψις : σκήπτω
σκοπέω : σκέπτομαι
σπέρμα : σπείρω
σπονδή : σπένδω
σποράς : σπείρω
σταθμός : ἵστημι
στάσις : ἵστημι
στέμμα : στέφω
στεναγμός : στένω
στήλη : στέλλω
στίγμα : στίζω
στόνος : στένω
στροφή : στρέφω
σύμβολον : βάλλω
συμπόσιον : πίνω
σύμπτωμα : πίπτω
συμφορά : φέρω
συνήγορος : ἀγείρω
συνθήκη : τίθημι
συνουσία : εἰμί
σύντομος : τέμνω

σφαγή : σφάττω
σχεδόν : ἔχω
σχέτλιος : ἔχω
σχῆμα : ἔχω
σχολή : ἔχω
σωτήρ : σῶος
σώφρων : σῶος

T

τάλαντον : τάλας
τάφος : θάπτω
τάφρος : θάπτω
τεθνάναι : θνῄσκω
τέκνον : τίκτω
τελευτή : τέλος
τηλικόσδε : ἧλιξ
τήμερον : ἡμέρα
τιμωρέω : τιμή
τλήμων : τάλας
τμῆμα : τέμνω
τοῖχος : τεῖχος
τόκος : τίκτω
τόλμα : τάλας
τομή : τέμνω
τόνος : τείνω
τότε : ὁ
τράπεζα : πέδον
τραυματίζω : τιτρώσκω
τρίπους : πέδον
τρίχινος : θρίξ
τρόπαιον : τρέπω
τρόπος : τρέπω
τρόχος : τρέχω
τροφός : τρέφω
τύχη : τυγχάνω

Y

ὕπατος : ὑπέρ
ὑπήκοος : ἀκούω
ὑπηρέτης : ἐρέττω
ὑπισχνέομαι : ἔχω
ὑπόδημα : δέω
ὑποζύγιον : ζεύγνυμι
ὑπόθεσις : τίθημι
ὑποθήκη : τίθημι
ὑποπτεύω : ὄψις
ὕπουργος : ἔργον
ὗς : σῦς
ὕφασμα : ὑφαίνω

140

Φ

φαρέτρα : φέρω
φάσκω : φημί
φθόγγος : φθέγγομαι
φθορά : φθείρω
φόρος : φέρω
φρονέω : φρήν
φροντίς : φρήν
φρουρά : ὁράω
φυγάς : φεύγω
φυγή : φεύγω
φωνή : φημί
φώρ : φέρω

Χ

χαρά : χαίρω
χαρακτήρ : χαράττω
χαρίεις : χαίρω

χάρις : χαίρω
χερρόνησος : νῆσος
χιών : χειμών
χόω : χέω
χρεών : χρῶ
χρήζω : χρῶ
χρῆμα : χρῶ
χρήσιμος : χρῶ
χρησμός : χρῶ
χρηστός : χρῶ
χύτρα : χέω
χῶσις : χέω

Ω

ᾠδή : ᾄδω
ὡς : ὅς
ὥστε : ὅς
ὠφελέω : ὄφελος

DATE DUE